"Learn how to see. Realize that everything
connects to everything else."
— Leonardo da Vinci

"The difference between the right word and
the almost right word is the difference between
lightening and the lightening bug."
— Mark Twain

"In union, there is strength."
— Aesop

THE TRILOGY OF
YES

Connection, Communication, & Cooperation

A Trilogy of Sales Skills
that Inspire Customers to Say Yes

Andy Olen

NORTH HALL PARTNERS LLC
WHITEFISH BAY, WISCONSIN

The Trilogy of Yes: Connection, Communication, & Cooperation: A Trilogy of Sales Skills that Inspire Customers to Say Yes
Copyright © 2017 Andy Olen.

First Edition

While the author has made every effort to provide accurate Internet addresses at the time of publication, the author does not assume any responsibility for errors or for changes that occur after publication. Further, the author does not have any control over and does not assume responsibility for third-party websites or their content.

ISBN: 978-0-9986752-0-6
Library of Congress Control Number: 2017902008

Editing: Carolyn Kott Washburne
Cover Design: Andrea & Stefan, www.artbiro.ba
Interior Design: Kate Hawley by Design
Proofreading: Paula Haubrich

Printed in the United States of America

Books may be purchased in quantity, with a volume rebate, and/or special sales through the website www.TrilogyOfYes.com or email to Andy@TrilogyOfYes.com

Published by: North Hall Partners LLC, Whitefish Bay, Wisconsin

To my loving family—
Melanie, Ainsley, Audrey, and Anderson

The Great Authors and Motivators in the Olen Family—
Dale, Joelyn, and Amy

And my friends and mentors in business who gave me
the opportunity to experiment and create

Table of Contents

Introduction

A Trilogy: a series of three related works of art, each piece of art able to stand on its own, and when combined, the three together have the power to produce a masterpiece.

Selling is an art. The best sales artists deploy a trilogy of skills that propel them to the top of the sales profession. Salespeople are architects of connection, orators of communication, and sculptors of cooperation. By using these skills, they transform the first encounter with a customer into a long-term partnership rich with trust and teamwork. Their collection of art is inventoried by the breadth and depth of relationships they build with customers. The value of their relationships is monetized by loyal customers saying YES time and time again. *The Trilogy of Yes* is a guide for all salespeople to create winning and profitable customer partnerships.

The sales Trilogy of connection, communication, and cooperation inspires customers to say YES. YES to having the next meeting, YES to accepting a bid, YES to negotiating, YES to buying, and YES to developing a long-term partnership. Most importantly, they say YES to you. As in life, we seek to help and support the people we are invested in and care about. The great sales artists build similar relationships with their customers. Once developed, customers reciprocate their support back to the salesperson. Both the salesperson and the customer become motivated to help the other succeed. Everything is possible when this relationship exists.

My sales teams and I have sold over $1 billion of products and services over the last 10 years. I've cheered on salespeople across industries and around the globe who successfully deploy connectivity, communication, and cooperation with their customers. It doesn't matter if you are selling a simple solution to a common problem or a complex solution to an unmet need, the sales principles detailed in this book will help you become a more effective and more successful salesperson.

This book is written for salespeople looking to take their performance to the next level. This book offers insights for sales managers looking to become better coaches. This book serves as a call to action to human resource leaders who write the job descriptions for salespeople and sales leaders. These pages are for the general managers and executives who run businesses that depend on talented salespeople to represent the company's products.

When sales leaders and talent managers recruit, and hire salespeople who can create bonds, can thoughtfully express themselves, and can harness the power of teamwork, customers win. Create winning, lasting, and loyal customer relationships that give your brands the winning edge.

The sales skills of connecting, communicating, and cooperating all work together—no one skill more important than the other. Salespeople who excel at all three skills generate loyalty and enthusiasm from their customers. A customer's loyalty is returned to the salesperson in the form of product purchases.

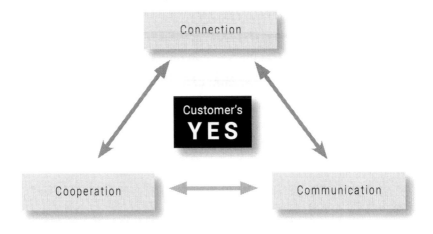

This book is organized in two parts. Part 1 introduces the three sales skills in The Trilogy of Yes:

1. *Connect* – Create a link between you and the customer that marks the start of the relationship.
2. *Communicate* – Discover your customer's challenges and articulate how you will provide a solution.
3. *Cooperate* – Form a team with your customer that creates win-win solutions for all parties.

Part 2 applies The Trilogy of Yes skills across the three phases of the sales cycle. These customer-focused phases are:

1. *The Dating Phase* – meeting, listening, and connecting with your customer as a new relationship forms.
2. *The Trading Phase* – cooperatively negotiating the terms of the sale and leading the customer to say YES to your product.
3. *The Partnering Phase* – enabling long-term and repeatable selling success with your customer.

Executing The Trilogy of Yes skills across the sales cycle will create explosive and durable results.

It takes commitment, practice, and a disciplined mindset to welcome and use *The Trilogy of Yes* approach. The good news is that we practice relationship skills in both work and in life, and in many ways, sales parallels life. Therefore, your Trilogy of Yes training has already begun. Master The Trilogy of Yes in sales and win more. Usher the Trilogy's learnings and practices into your daily life and enjoy the benefits of stronger relationships with friends and family.

Humans survive and thrive with cooperation that is facilitated by communication and enriched through authentic connections between people. Create lasting partnerships and unlock sales greatness.

Part 1

THE TRILOGY OF YES SALES SKILLS

Salespeople who connect with their customers, who effectively communicate, and who actively cooperate sell more. A good salesperson selling great products and solutions creates customer value. Alex, the salesman at the running store, spent 20 minutes with the customer to find the right marathon shoe for her. Kristin, the real estate agent, worked closely with the young parents to find the best home for their growing family. Good salespeople help customers make smart decisions. When the customer wins, the salesperson wins too. Salespeople who constantly make it to the top of the sales rankings have a common trait: they build great relationships with their customers. Customers seek their help to make important and informed decisions.

In the digital era, salespeople will continue to sell products directly to customers. In fact, interpersonal selling skills that create durable relationships are more critical today than ever before. Think about it: at the click of a button, your customers have access to the specifications, price, and reviews of any product in the world. They connect on Facebook to friends who have posted comments and shared opinions about your products. Access to information and peer influence leave today's customer more powerful than ever before.

Technology will continue to aid the customer, so salespeople must continuously improve their selling skills to keep up with well-informed customers. Salespeople who excel at connecting, communicating, and cooperating will both level the playing field and enjoy a competitive sales advantage.

Part 1 of *The Trilogy of Yes* examines connecting, communicating, and cooperating. You will discover why these skills work and how to put them into action with your customers.

Chapter 1

The Power of Connection

"Invisible threads are the strongest ties." — *Friedrich Nietzsche*

We crave connection. Connecting is important to our health and well-being.

A study showed that strong social connections lead to an improved rate of survival.[1]

A study of college students found that young adults built stronger immune systems when they had a broader social network and deeper connections with others.[2]

We derive happiness from rich and deep relationships. Laughing with friends, getting a wave from your daughter as she sings with her school chorus, and the embrace of a loved one create warmth and joy. The benefits of forming strong and healthy connections in life are clear. Unfortunately, the opposite is true as well. Living a life without connection has negative consequences for our health. The risk of Alzheimer's disease and dementia increase in people who are less connected. There are higher rates of anxiety and depression in people less bonded to others. Researchers found that social rejection impacts the brain in the same manner a body injury does. Both events create physical pain.[3]

Alarmingly, connectivity trends are not working in our favor. Connections appear to be on the decline. A study showed that from 1985 to 2004, the average American dropped from having three confidants to only one. A confidant is another person you share important insights with. Moreover,

25 percent of Americans identified as having no confidants at all. The study found that by 2004, a growing number of Americans were isolated and "shut off" from others.[4]

To live happier and healthier lives, we need to work to maintain meaningful connections with people. In sales, establishing a connection, or link, with the customer remains paramount in reducing customers' buying fears, establishing trust, and, most importantly, inspiring them to say YES. We say YES to people we have a genuine connection with. Customers say YES to salespeople they connect with and who are confident will offer a solution to the challenges they face.

I learned a valuable sales lesson in the power of connection in an unlikely place, a college calculus class. I have my bachelor of arts (BA) degree from the University of Wisconsin-Madison. I chose the BA degree, in part, because it didn't require any math classes. My math skills went on vacation somewhere between my junior and senior years of high school. However, fate would deal me a devilish hand a few years later. I chose to return to Wisconsin to study and earn a master's degree in business. My focus was finance, and a prerequisite for finance students was two semesters of calculus. I had six months to get both semesters of calculus done before business classes started. It was time to jump back into math.

Ironically, I fell in love with math after my six-month intensive study. Today I wouldn't be able to find the antiderivative of a function, yet I walked away from my advanced calculus class with a powerful lesson I apply with customers: there is nothing more powerful than the "=" sign. From math to sales, here's how it happened.

The advanced calculus class was taught by Wisconsin professor and mathematician Robert Wilson. Professor Wilson is a wizard. On his website, he even shares statistics that chart out the best months of the year to give birth to a famous mathematician. He is committed to the numbers.

Although I recall the hard work and complex problem sets from his class, what I remember most about Professor Wilson was that he was the advocate-in-chief of a certain math symbol. He preached the power of the equal sign,

"=", two powerful parallel lines. He said one day, "Friends, there is nothing more powerful in the world than the equal sign. It links everything together. When you voice that something is equal, you are making a deeply profound statement and connection." He never deviated from his equal sign evangelism. If a student responded and said, "It might be equal," Professor Wilson would quickly assert, "You really need to be careful throwing around comments like that. Remember, when you say equal, that means equal. It is not debatable, end of discussion. The equal sign unites. It says these two are the same."

Professor Wilson was right. The equal sign is all-powerful. I have carried Professor Wilson's enthusiasm into sales, and I regularly apply the equal sign lesson to selling activities. I actively attempt to find common connections—equal signs—between myself and the customer. Similarities create trusting bonds. Developing trust early in a customer relationship accelerates the selling cycle, facilitates effective communication, and sparks cooperation. Quickly discover a common fact, trait, or passion that links you to the customer.

Salesperson		Customer
"I love the Cubs!"	=	"Me, too. I went to Game Four of the World Series."
"I think we might have gone to the same elementary school."	=	"We did! Did you have Ms. Walden for first grade?"

As soon as you hear the customer say, "Wow, we have a lot in common," the relationship is off to a good start. Find out what you both have in common and leverage this connection to ease the fears and anxieties of a new customer engagement. Let the equal sign work its power for you.

Connecting Helps Overcome Misconceptions and Fears

Connecting with the customer may not be the first action that comes to mind when you think of a new buyer and seller relationship. Some say the first step with a customer is to find out what his needs are. I argue it's premature for this discovery to take place at the outset of the relationship. The customer will begin to reveal his needs as a connection with the salesperson forms.

In reality, at face value, the buyer and seller begin their relationship with an adversarial posture and bias. Customers have adversarial thoughts about salespeople and the sales process that have been formed from common stereotypes. These concerns include:

> "I need to fight the salesperson to get the best price."
> "I am being sold a bill of goods."
> "I've been lied to before and paid a price."
> "He is too salesy." (I have come to interpret "salesy" to mean: slick, slimy, and smooth. None of these adjectives is helpful.)

Customers often enter the sales cycle anxious about parts of the sales process, such as the negotiation. Internally they tell themselves, "If I don't press this salesperson hard and fight for the truth at every turn, I might get ripped off." Fear leads to defensiveness, and defensiveness leads to conflict. Conflict has the power to push the customer away from the salesperson. A connection is not achievable when conflict holds the relationship hostage.

The salesperson also begins the new relationship with concerns and misgivings about the customer sitting across the table.

> "All the customer cares about is price. Nothing more."
> "He is blinded by what the competition says."
> "He won't give me access to the other stakeholders in the account."
> "If I don't make this sale now, I will miss my quota!"
> "He is too slow to make a final purchase decision!"

I contend it doesn't need to be like this. These stereotypes and feelings act as inhibitors that handicap the creation of winning solutions on both sides of the table. Thus, the salesperson's ability to facilitate and establish a connection with the customer becomes a critical early step in the sales cycle. The warmth and comfort of a connection helps customers overcome fears.

How to Create Powerful Connections

Your goal is to discover and establish a common link between yourself and the customer. This link secures the keystone in the foundation of the relationship. Around the keystone, a strong and durable relationship can be built. There are three best practices to use to establish a link with the customer:

1. Be curious,
2. Be authentic and genuine, and
3. Be prepared.

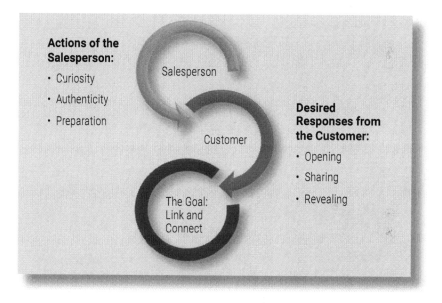

I've had the opportunity to connect with customers around the world. It doesn't matter the culture or the country, connections are key to creating the first sale.

Curiosity Creates the Link

Great salespeople have genuine and endless curiosity. They are interested in their customers' lives, including their hobbies, families, and vacation destinations. They search for the customers' motivation to buy. They know how customers earn a bonus. They identify the important stakeholders in the buying process.

Curious salespeople ask a lot of questions. They, knowingly or unknowingly, deploy the Socratic method. Socrates, the Greek philosopher, used questions to seek out the truth. Lawyers are taught the Socratic method of questioning witnesses. Good first dates in life are usually filled with hundreds of questions going back and forth between the daters as they get to know each other.

Through curiosity and question-asking, the salesperson can find a common link shared with the customer. Finding a common link is like a foot that wedges the door open. It helps you open the conversation and engage the customer. Links can be formed on a wide-ranging set of topics such as family, hometowns, favored sports teams, shared hobbies, and favorite restaurants. The goal is to discover a link with the customer on a fact or experience that is meaningful to him. If the link is that you both like McDonald's food, that is okay, but it's not a penetrating discovery. If you discover that your kids go to the same school, that's more personal and profound. A personal or family connection accelerates trust as the salesperson and customer discover they share common values. Focus your curiosity and questions on discovering a powerful link with your customer.

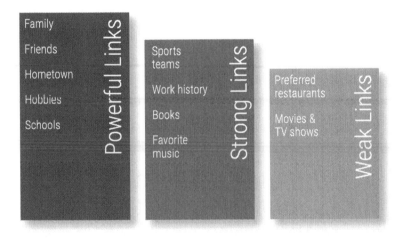

Curiosity doesn't stop after the first meeting, so over time, continue to explore and discover new links with the customer. Your curiosity will create new and lasting connections.

A Little Authenticity Goes a Long Way

Authenticity and genuineness engender trust. I value genuine people because I have a truer sense of what motivates them and the values they hold that shape their actions. I evaluate whether my core values and beliefs are similar. If my values align to theirs, a partnership may develop.

In 1997, I wrote my bachelor's thesis about how a candidate's image in a presidential election was becoming an impactful determinant of how people vote. If I were rewriting my thesis today, I would take out candidate "image" and replace it with "authenticity," because increasingly, authenticity shapes how Americans vote for president of the United States. Ronald Reagan and Barack Obama were two politicians who used authenticity to their advantage. Reagan was a natural showman and used humor and jokes to ease the mood. Obama's natural oratory skills were true to his life story. Both individuals connected, and millions said YES to their candidacies.

Some politicians have run into "authenticity" trouble. Al Gore kept changing his clothes and tone to try and connect with voters in the 2000 campaign. It didn't work. In 2016, the media stated, "We still don't know who the real Hillary is." These two candidates labored to genuinely connect with others and transmit authenticity. Although many factors led to their defeat, an enthusiasm gap was common between these two politicians and their opponents. I attribute their enthusiasm gaps to the challenges they faced in authentically connecting with voters.

People recognize when they are engaging a "fake" person. It's a discouraging feeling. We walk away from the interaction not sure what the other person believes. We don't know his true feelings. We are suspicious of his motives. A customer enters the sales process already fearful on some level. If a customer senses she is working with a salesperson who is fake, or "salesy," her fear will increase, and she will likely turn elsewhere for a connection and solution.

Trust is established through authenticity. My mom shared with me the best definition of trust that I've heard: trust is based on **consistency** and **predictability**. Being predictably consistent creates a clear window into who you are as a person. The opposite runs true as well. When a person is inconsistent and unpredictable, I struggle to form a bond with this individual. Authenticity becomes evasive when trust fails.

Each human personality is unique. Some of us are extroverts who love to be in a crowd of people. We feed off people's energy and open ourselves up. The opposite of an extrovert is an introvert. Introverts are awesome listeners. However, it takes introverts a little longer to open up to others.

In life, we encounter people whom we disagree with, or with whom we have an opposing point of view. One bridge that unites our unique personalities is trust. Trust is the glue that creates productive bonds between people with different outlooks. I enjoy the challenge of working with customers who are consistently and predictably different than me. It's more difficult for me to work with customers who are inconsistent in their approach and behavior. If they are hot one day and cold the next, it is challenging to establish a trusting rhythm. The key to managing the hot and cold customer is to be prepared to flex either way as you engage him. Over time, your nimbleness and adjustment to his idiosyncrasies will create a rhythm that moves the relationship forward in a positive manner.

Putting the authentic you on display in front of your customer is a powerful sales skill. As customers sense your authenticity, they become more comfortable building trust with you. Once trusted, being able to extract the same level of authenticity from your customer in return creates dynamic connections. In these moments, you are breaking through to the core beliefs and values each of you holds sacred. Equal signs pop up everywhere as connections are made. A salesperson's authenticity has the power to connect and engender authenticity in return. The deeper and broader the connections are, the stronger the relationship between seller and buyer becomes.

A quick self-check can be done to determine your level of authenticity with a customer. Ask yourself the following questions:

"Do my customers actively engage with me when I clearly and passionately articulate the benefits of my product?"
"Am I consistent and predictable in my approach when I interact with my customers?" For example, is your energy level, engagement, and

mood consistent in each customer encounter? When a customer makes a request, do you follow up on a timely basis and insure he has the information he needs?

"Have I discovered and established new connections during each interaction with my customer?" Make it your goal to exit each customer encounter having created a new link between the two of you. As your customer opens up to you, the opportunity to find the deeper connection increases.

If you answered yes to these questions, you are deploying authenticity that will help create a lasting connection with the customer.

It's important to be comfortable in your own skin with the customer, comfortable with your own words, and comfortable connecting in your own way using your own style. The mantra in this book is "now go make it your own." Ultimately I want your personality to shine in front of the customer. There is nothing more authentic and connecting then sharing your personality with another person.

Preparation Creates the Confidence to Connect

I walk into every customer meeting prepared. I prepare by answering each of the following questions prior to the first meeting:

"What is the objective the meeting?"

"What is the customer's history with our company and products?"

"What are the important questions I need answered in order to prepare an offer?"

"What will the customer likely ask me?"

"What are the next steps after a successful meeting?"

My confidence grows through preparation. I am prepared to answer the customer's questions and put my competence on display.

When you are prepared, and the tough customer question is asked, it's likely you will be ready with an answer. When you are prepared, you control the direction of the conversation and exude confidence by giving crisp and thoughtful responses. You choose better words and are a better listener. Finally, you are able to anticipate what the customer will say next.

When unprepared, it shows, and the negative consequence is that your true personality is blocked from the customer. When I am caught not having a solution or answer to a basic customer request, my mind starts racing, my eyes wander as I'm thinking, and I tighten up just a bit. As I search for answers, I don't listen as well, and anxiety creeps in. My mouth goes dry as I hunt for words to fill the dead air. Remember when you didn't study hard for a test in school? A question pops up on the exam that you have no clue how to answer. That is the same feeling I have when I am underprepared for a customer meeting. Preparation eliminates that anxious feeling. Preparation allows me to run my plan and transmit confidence and calmness to the customer. I am able to establish deeper connections when I am prepared versus scared.

Remaining Thoughtful While Connecting

The Trilogy of Yes connection lives through human-to-human interaction. Salespeople must exercise strong emotional intelligence and avoid showstopper conversations that may contain opinions that push the customer away. Also, a strong and bonding connection is not generated by simply "LinkingIn" with a customer or following her on social media. Nor have I ever met a good salesperson whose pathway to success was paved solely by building a large following on Twitter or Instagram. The Trilogy of Yes approach relies on the time-tested method of meeting with, talking with, and connecting with the customer. The bonds of loyalty and long-term partnership require connections and emotions to be shared in person between the salesperson and the customer. Thus, it's important to hone the skills of personal interactions to facilitate an open and comfortable exchange of insights and ideas that lead to a meaningful connection.

Emotional Intelligence

Activate your emotional intelligence while building a connection with the customer. Emotional intelligence is an individual's awareness of and reaction to another person's emotions. This important skill informs our actions and responses to a customer's request or opinion. For example, if we confuse authenticity with indiscriminate self-disclosure, we may be in for some tough sledding. Here's an example where the salesperson is NOT deploying emotional intelligence:

> *Salesperson:* "How was your weekend?"
>
> *Customer:* "It was great. We really enjoyed the nice weather. How about you?"
>
> *Salesperson:* "I had an interesting weekend. I skinny dipped in Lake Michigan and was fined by the police for indecent exposure."

TMI—Too Much Information. Yes, the salesperson is being open and authentic. However, this is not the time or place to divulge this type of information. A connection won't likely be made after this exchange.

Rather, emotional intelligence guides the salesperson to have this type of conversation with the customer:

> *Salesperson:* "How was your weekend?"
>
> *Customer:* "It was great. We really enjoyed the nice weather. How about you?"
>
> *Salesperson:* "I had a good weekend too. I spent the day at the beach and soaked in the sun."

Apply professional filters to discussions with customers. Discuss safe and neutral topics such as hometowns, favorite teams, and families. As the relationship builds, work in deeper questions to get at the positive and negative emotions that may exist for your products and the buying process. Finally, stay away from attempting the "showstopper connection."

Showstopper Connection: Politics and Religion

Although tempting, do not try to establish a connection with a customer on political and religious views. Politics, religion, hot social issues, and how much money you make are high-risk connection topics. Now, you may be saying,

"Andy, you are telling me to be myself, so shouldn't these topics be on the table? If the customer and I agree, we connect." Yes, this is a true statement if you are confident every customer you visit shares your views. If you are not 100 percent sure, don't find out the tough way. In my opinion, it's not worth the risk.

Showstopper Connection: Harsh Talk about the Competition

Having cut my sales teeth in the medical equipment market, I learned quickly that trashing the competition wasn't a good way to create a connection. My competitors' products were approved by regulatory agencies around the world as safe and effective products to be used in treating humans. Clinicians use their trained judgment to choose which product is best given the patient and the situation. Expressing an opinion to a doctor that her product preference is "bad" questions her clinical judgment. It's hard to establish a connection if you are attacking your customer's decisions.

Don't Be Mistaken—Social Media Doesn't Count as a Connection

Connecting on social media is not the type of connection-building that will inspire your customer to say YES to your sales offer. I appreciate and use LinkedIn, yet I don't fool myself into believing that I have a deep connection with the people I follow. There may be 1,000-plus people you're "connected" to, but it doesn't mean any of these people would buy something from you on this connection alone. Social media is a tool to learn about and stay in touch with people. In no way is social media a substitute for the authentic and meaningful connections you are seeking to build.

As we work through the three phases of The Trilogy of Yes sales cycle, I'll provide best practices on how to navigate social media and your customer relationships. Strong and durable connections are best made in person. Hear the tone and inflection of your customer's voice. Observe body language and facial expressions to evaluate how effectively you are connecting. Strong connections are made face-to-face, not on Snapchat.

Create a Meaningful Connection with Your Customer

Connecting with your customer creates a link and a bond. The more powerful the link, the more quickly you move the relationship forward. The customer's fear of and anxiety about the "slick" salesperson is eased when common values and experiences are shared. A salesperson's curiosity and question-asking identify a link. Authenticity deployed through consistency and predictability, develops trust. The salesperson's preparation before each meeting creates confidence. With confidence, the salesperson relaxes, listens, and connects with the customer. As discussed previously, we know being connected is good for our mental and physical health. By developing connections with your customers, you are literally making them healthier people. In addition, you increase the odds your customer will say YES to you and your products.

Chapter 2

The Power of Communication

"Think like a wise man, but communicate in the language of the people."
— *William Butler Yeats*

The most important sales tool we have is our voice. We communicate through words, and body language. Strong and effective communication with your customer will fast track a YES to you.

Communication and language have benefited my sales teams. Teaching salespeople how to communicate effectively with customers is rewarding because the positive impact is often immediate. There is no sweeter compliment than someone saying, "Andy, I used the words you taught me with my customer and it worked! He said YES." Being a good communicator is not an innate skill, it is developed with time and practice.

A little bit of observation goes a long way in becoming an effective sales communicator. The next time someone says something to you that elicits a reaction, take a mental note of that experience. What words and body language did the person use that influenced your response? The same exercise should be done when you notice that your words and body language elicit an emotional reaction, either positive or negative, from a customer. By observing and pondering these experiences, you will notice certain trends. When you say "x," you usually receive "y" feedback. I've taught communication skills classes to graduate business students, and I share best practices with them that are applicable to sales. The communication approach I teach forms an acronym, POPS:

Preparation

Optimism

Passion

Self-Awareness

Be **P**repared for every important interaction. Convey **O**ptimism that progress will be made. Be **P**assionate about providing a helpful solution. Choose words, tones, and body language that are natural to you, and make it your own. **S**elf-Awareness keeps you in your comfort zone. POPS has helped me connect and cooperate with customers. Practice POPS, and your communication skills will become a powerful sales and relationship creator.

The second sales skill of The Trilogy of Yes is the salesperson's ability to maximize communication that moves the customer to YES. This chapter suggests words, body language, and best practices to use with customers. I will share simple communication tactics that I have used and have taught salespeople that establish and deepen customer relationships.

Selling Power Words

Master the following words with your customers: "Yes" "I can" "If" "Together" "We" "Win."

The winning words are easy to remember. They form a fun sentence when strung together:

YES I CAN IF TOGETHER WE WIN

These are small words that deliver big results. These are Selling Power Words that, when used with a customer, facilitate positive action. These words have the power to pull the customer closer to you, and your product offering.

YES Is Affirming

We are on a mission to move our customer into position to say YES, and to achieve this, salespeople serve as role models for the customer. By using the word YES frequently with your customer, you model the language and words you hope to hear in return. People mimic and repeat words that are positive, resonate, and strike a constructive tone when voiced and heard. When you repeatedly say YES to the customer, you encourage a YES in return. YES is a cooperative word that signals two people are in agreement. There is acknowledgment of the customer's needs when you use it in reply to a request. We also emote with the word YES. Think about how YES is used in daily life and how it harnesses a larger emotion.

> "Yes!" The celebration starts as the winning shot is made in Game 7 and the fans scream out in joy.
> "Yes," a teary-eyed partner says in response to a marriage proposal.
> "Yes, I will look at the details of the analysis," the CEO says to the senior vice president who is pitching an acquisition.
> "Yes, you can have a birthday party. Who would you like to have over to the party?" a dad says to his daughter who wants to have her best friends celebrate the big day with her.
> "Yes, we are interested in your skill set and experiences. Would you be able to come to the home office for an interview?" the recruiter says to the candidate.

YES is a Selling Power Word that creates forward movement and positive emotions.

"I Can" Is Commitment, Credibility, Cooperation

I vividly remember that my high school's cross-country team wore shirts with the quote, "If you say you can't, you won't. If you say you can, you might." "I CAN" delivers three beneficial "Cs" to the customer:

1. Commitment: to act on the request made by the customer.
2. Credibility: to deliver on the request made by the customer.
3. Cooperation: to form a team with the customer.

Every time I say "I can" to a customer, I see him relax and smile. The reaction signals that the customer's voice has been heard and empowered. There is a bond that forms when a salesperson responds with an "I can" to a customer's request. The salesperson commits to taking her time and energy, deploying it to try to advance the customer's request. The bonds of commitment to one another deepen when commitments are made. In these moments, the customer sees the salesperson as a partner rather than as a seller.

At this point, you may be wondering, "Well, I can't say 'I can' to everything because I might get caught not being able to deliver on the commitment." That's right, it is possible to "I can" yourself out of a sale by overcommitting and under-delivering. Here's a tactic I use in nearly every new customer engagement to ensure that I am safe in making "I can" commitments without the risk of under-delivering. I deploy the following sentence: "I will do the best I can to answer every question you have. If I don't know the answer to a question or request, the good news is I know the person in the company who has the answer."

This sentence is strong on two fronts: 1) you express to your customer that you don't have ALL the answers, and you are connected to the resources who do—this showcases your credibility and solution-oriented approach to the customer; 2) you can come back to this line when faced with a question you are unsure how to answer throughout the sales cycle.

For example, if a customer wants to know about a specific technical aspect of your product and you aren't 100 percent sure, say, "I want to give you the right answer. As I shared with you earlier, I know the person who built that functionality. Let me ask him." Perfect. The customer appreciates that you did not "b.s." him with some made-up answer. He sees that you are a connected person in the company and your credibility will grow.

"I can," and its powerful cousins "I will" and "I do," are energizing words. In sales and in life, these action-oriented words encourage cooperative teamwork.

"If": A Little Word with Big Power

"If" is a word that takes on a lot of different applications in our language. In sales, "if" serves as an elegant word for salespeople to use to maintain a fair and equitable negotiation. "If" signals a condition in a trade: I'll give you this "if" you give me that. In sales, we trade a product or service for money. I use "if" throughout the negotiating process to ask for value in return from my customer, "Yes, I can sell the product at the price you requested, if you buy two."

"Together" and "We" Are Partnership Words

Recall the famous TEAM acronym "*Together* Everyone Achieves More." As you build your relationship with the customer, use the word "together" to verbalize the team dynamic that is forming.

> "I am excited to take this new journey together."
> "Together we can make this happen."
> "My hope is to build a lasting partnership together."

In life, we use the word and sentiment "together" in all of our meaningful relationships.

> "We'll get through this together."
> "I'd like us to work on this together."
> "We've been together for 10 years."

I want you to have long-term and rewarding relationships with your customers. There will be tough moments along with the good moments as you navigate the customer relationship through time. Always step toward and move forward together with your customer.

"We" and "together" are the peanut butter and jelly of partnership words. "We" is a team pronoun. By definition, "we" can't just be one person. When salespeople use "we," they bind themselves to the customer.

> "We will figure this out."
> "How can we create a win-win?"
> "We both want this to be successful."

In life, "we" is used to rally and act.

> "We wanted it more!"
> "We can do this."
> "I believe we will win."

Everyone Wants to "Win"

"Win" is a Selling Power Word. It's important to deploy "win" in the context of generating a win for your customer. As you work on behalf of bettering your customer, she has a better chance to win with your solution. A customer may earn a large bonus by buying a product that helps the business exceed expectations. A customer may be rewarded with a promotion and public recognition when the newly purchased software product saves the company money. If the salesperson can turn the product into a success for the customer, the customer, not the salesperson, deserves the credit. Allow winning language to inspire and create success for your customer.

"My goal is to help create a win for your company."

"How can I help turn this opportunity into a big win for you?"

"I want you to receive the recognition you deserve for making great progress."

As in the movies, there are good guys and bad guys. We have identified the good sales words. Let's look at the bad sales words.

Words to Eliminate with Your Customer

Eliminate the following words from *all* customer conversations, "Yeah, but," "Always," "Never," "Everyone."

To make the bad words easy to remember they form a sentence that reminds you to not use them with customers:

NEVER "YEAH BUT" EVERYONE ALWAYS

Ouch, they are even tough to write. Let's start with "Yeah, but."

Are You a "Yeah But-er"?

Listen to yourself speak in everyday conversations. Do you find yourself saying "Yeah, but" a lot? Do you say "but" often? I cringe when I hear these words spoken to me because it means that the speaker believes my opinion was untenable. On top of that, I heard a flippant "Yeah" to kick things off. "Yeah" is usually accompanied by an eye roll or a hand extended signaling "STOP speaking!" To the listener, these two words sound condescending when spoken together.

Traveling the globe many times over, I have found that "Yeah, but" is a worldwide linguistic phenomenon. As a sales leader doing business reviews with sales managers and sales representatives, I listened to the language the team used. No matter the language or culture, "Yeah, but" pops up everywhere.

Andy: "It doesn't appear the customer is ready to order. I don't think this deal will close this month."
Salesperson: "Yeah, but the customer said it was going to happen."

Andy: "I believe the customer is trying to get you to lower the price of the product without providing any value in return."
Salesperson: "Yeah, but he said he doesn't have any more money in the budget to pay the offered price."

Andy: "You don't have enough activity listed on your call plan to generate the leads needed to close the quota this quarter."
Salesperson: "Yeah, but most customers are out on vacation this week. I can't reach them."

"Yeah, but" lurks around our personal lives too. I am a father of three pre-adolescent kids. I have at least three "Yeah, but" conversations each day. "Yeah, but I don't want to go." "Yeah, but let me just watch the end of this show first." "Yeah, but all the other kids have a cell phone." "Yeah, but my friends don't have to." Kids are savvy, and they learn the "Yeah, but" approach from us. Why? Because we use it all the time. Take a listen.

I have become so sensitized to "Yeah, but" language that I now stop the conversation the minute I hear it deployed. I try nicely to say, "I'm sorry, I am not good at "Yeah, but" conversations. Is there a way we can make this more constructive?"

Here's a customer "Yeah, but" example. You'll get the sense fast that this type of communication is not effective, and when you start to use "but" with your customer, he will likely use "but" with you. Thus, a discussion with many "buts" begins a communication death spiral.

Customer: "I really like the feature the competitor has."

Salesperson: "Yeah, but my other customer told me it doesn't work well."

Customer: "Okay, my point is that it is a feature that would add value."

Salesperson: "Yeah, but it's one of the reasons why that product is more expensive than my product."

Customer: "I hear you, but what I am looking for is a solution that offers me certain features your competitor has."

Salesperson: "Yeah, but we have been working together for so long. Why would you switch? I thought we had a close relationship."

Customer: "Yeah, but our relationship was based on mutual understanding and cooperation. For whatever reason, we seem to be heading down the wrong path today."

This salesperson is about to "Yeah, but" himself out of a sale. If you use uncooperative language with your customer, you are creating obstacles that will limit your ability to win the deal.

"But" is the anti-cooperation word. The definition of "but" literally means to pivot away from a point or position just stated to a counter position. In the extreme, "but" is used to start an argument. You could substitute the following sentence in for the word "but" and express the same uncooperative point: "There is no way what you said is true or accurate." When you say "but," be ready for the other party to become defensive.

Although it's hard to do, I am trying to eliminate "but" from my vocabulary. Replacing "but" with "and" is a good habit to form, "It was warm this morning, and I'm pretty sure it will get cooler tonight." My challenge to you is to eliminate "Yeah, but" from all conversations with customers. Take it one step further: try to reduce the use of "but" by replacing it with "and."

Extreme Words that Challenge Credibility

I was never a great standardized test whiz. Although I did well on the essay part of the GMAT (business school entrance exam), the scoring on that section was only window dressing and didn't count in the overall result.

The dreaded Integrated Reasoning, Verbal, and Quant sections, unfortunately, did count. When I studied for the exam, I remember hearing the following advice: when an answer to a question contained extreme words like "always" or "never," the answer should be eliminated. The world doesn't work in extremes. Can you think of a situation, event, or phenomenon that is ALWAYS, NEVER, or EVERYONE? I can think of only a few, which are voiced by people you may have heard of:

> "Always go to other people's funerals, otherwise they won't come to yours." — Yogi Berra
> "Never say never." — Charles Dickens
> "We can't help everyone, but everyone can help someone." — Ronald Reagan

Let's look at examples of ALWAYS, NEVER, and EVERYONE in action with customers, and the negative response these words may elicit:

Salesperson: "The competition ALWAYS has long customer care wait times."
Customer: "Always? Hmmmm. They seem to respond faster than you."

Salesperson: "I've NEVER done that before!"
Customer: "Then you clearly aren't empowered to create a solution for me today."

Salesperson: "EVERYONE uses my product!"
Customer: "No way! Everyone?!"

ALWAYS, NEVER, and EVERYONE create an unproductive back-and-forth. I attempt to pivot conversations that use these words because they represent unrealistic scenarios. A psychologist friend of mine encouraged me to teach my kids *not* to use these words in describing feelings and situations. ALWAYS, NEVER, and EVERYONE take a discussion to an extreme and don't help build credibility for the salesperson in front of the customer.

Body Language Amplifies Your Words

I am an expressive. I wear my emotions and my feelings on my face. Colleagues that have worked with me know when I am excited and when I am concerned. I have worked on moderating my mood elevator to stay somewhere between the lobby level and the fifth floor. I avoid displaying wild enthusiasm and intense frustration. I am also working on modulating my body language so my words and my expressions match. Staying within a reasonable emotional range is a good leadership trait to exhibit in front of the customer. Connection and cooperation accelerate when words and body language align.

Body language, including facial expressions, mannerisms, and posture, are as powerful as the words we speak to our customers. Sunken shoulders, a pout, and a frown convey unhappiness. Crossed arms signal that defensive shields are being raised to protect us from what is being said. Slouching and being easily distracted sends an "I'm not interested message" to the receiver.

A forward lean, a listening ear, a smile, and a nodding head convey positive and engaged communication. Selling Power Words, combined with connecting and cooperative body language, are effective tools for the salesperson. Thoughtful body language will ease tensions, build trust, and encourage teamwork.

Words and Body Language in Play at a Sales Convention

I attended SalesForce.com's Dreamforce conference, and was blown away at the awesome and broad community the SalesForce.com brand has created. The convention was a place where salespeople like me came in from all over the globe to be sold new customer relationship management software. With hundreds of booths and thousands of salespeople selling high-tech solutions, I was excited to attend. I anticipated that the salespeople at Dreamforce would be some of the best I met. These are cutting-edge technologies and, shoot, we were at a convention where the primary goal was to sell salespeople new solutions (there is no tougher customer than a salesperson). I was ready to be dazzled by the sales masterminds and end up with a huge list of new apps I had to have.

What happened? The opposite! Many of the sales professionals I met had underdeveloped sales skills. As my initial surprise faded, I took a more curious approach to see what was happening. I pondered, "Was the software product that was being sold so good that salesmanship wasn't needed? Do these products sell themselves?" Maybe they were good enough for the time being. However, as in any industry, as competition increases, these products will need good salespeople to stand behind them.

I encountered the entire spectrum of sales communication at Dreamforce. I was drawn to salespeople who effectively used language to form a connection. When words and body language created confusion and frustration, the outcome turned negative quickly. As the sales leader turned customer, it was illuminating for me to watch these sellers communicate. The following examples serve as good case studies in sales communication.

Strong Sales Communication

I had a great tutorial on Service Cloud, SalesForce.com's customer service application, by a very thoughtful and smart SalesForce.com employee at the convention booth. She was highly inquisitive about the business challenges I faced. She was a subject matter expert yet did not make me feel unsmart. She smiled. She said, "I will" or "I can" to every follow-up question I asked. When she didn't have the answer to a question, she said, "I don't know, and I will find out and get back to you." Perfect.

Later in the day, my team and I met with two salespeople to learn more about their solution. We wanted to see the technology in action, and we felt that experiencing a demonstration was the best way to learn and evaluate. The two salespeople were fantastic. They booted up their computers. Logged onto the demonstration environment, and began walking through the functionality of the software. After each step of the demonstration, they turned to ask for feedback and take questions. Their body language was strong. High energy, passion for their work, and belief in the product all came through. We walked away liking the technology because it was a powerful solution advocated by two salespeople who used great verbal and nonverbal communication approaches to illustrate the strength of the application.

A Missed Opportunity to Effectively Communicate

I had the chance to meet with the founder of a software company at Dreamforce along with his head of sales. Their contract management software product had a positive reputation. The founder was a strong salesperson, and wanted to better understand why we were there to see him. He created an open environment. As the customer, I felt comfortable and began expressing my needs in a relaxed and open discussion.

Sitting behind the founder was his head of sales, who took a very different approach to the meeting. He was on his phone and was distracted by his inbound text messages. He would pop his head up every other minute and mutter "yup" or give a fake laugh to a comment where laughter wasn't required. His body language was distracting, and ultimately I passed on the product because the good work of the founder was washed away by his sales leader, who was all too ready to move on to the next appointment.

How Poor Communication Can Quickly Kill the Sale

The most unmemorable sales call of the conference took place in a hotel restaurant where we met with a software sales vice president. We were excited about his company's product. Unfortunately, the vice president of sales was unable to effectively communicate. A connection did not form and cooperation was nonexistent.

> *Andy:* "Would you be able to show us a demo of your software?"
>
> *Sales VP:* "I didn't realize you would want to see one today."
>
> *Andy:* "Yes. That is why we are here. We are visual learners."
>
> *Sales VP:* "It would be better for us to come to your office, and learn more about you before running a product demo."
>
> *Andy:* "That is not efficient for us. We are all here today. Can we do it now?"
>
> *Sales VP:* "Yeah, but the way our program works requires pre-configuration before a demo."
>
> *Andy:* "That sounds complex. Do you have a demo we can see?"

Sales VP: "Maybe I can get someone to see you at the booth. We are busy for the rest of the conference."

Andy: "We are going to decide soon on which product to select. Do you want to compete for our business?"

Sales VP: "Yeah, but it would be best if we came out to your office. We always do this first."

At this point, I decided to jump in to wrap up a sales conversation that ran into a dead end, "We are talking in a circle here. All we want to see is a demo. If that's not possible, it's a quick decision for us to not proceed with your software." The meeting rolled to a close. The sales vice president apologized that it didn't work, and my team agreed that was an example of how not to communicate.

Communication: The Ultimate Sales Tool

Communication is critical for connections to be made and cooperation to exist between salespeople and customers. We seek to connect with our words. We look to engender cooperation and excitement. The words we choose to speak are equally as important as the words we should eliminate. To amplify communication, our body language must match our words.

Connection and communication are two of The Trilogy of Yes sales skills. The third skill is cooperation. Let's examine the importance of building a cooperative team with the customer.

Chapter 3

The Power of Cooperation

"Individually we are one drop. Together, we are an ocean."
— *Ryunosuke Satoro*

Cooperating with your customer, like connecting, creates positive results because it's at the core of how we are wired as humans and how we prosper as a society. We have evolved and survive as a cooperative species. In fact, humanity's greatest triumphs were all cooperative endeavors:

The development of the iPod: engineers cooperated with marketers who cooperated with a visionary.

The first airplane: Orville and Wilbur Wright cooperated with one another to fly that plane in Kitty Hawk, North Carolina.

Restoring freedom to Europe in World War II: D-Day's five Normandy beaches were won through the bravery of cooperating and coordinating militaries.

Cooperation is a team event. It takes at least two people to form a team. A team has a common goal and works together. A good teammate holds sacred the best interests of the other team members. The basketball team's goal each time it possesses the ball is to score a basket. A play is run to set up a chance to score. One player brings the ball up the court. The forward sets a screen to free the dribbler. The center swings out to the free throw line as the defenders collapse on the guard heading to the basket. The guard floats the ball to the center, who has an open lane to the bucket and scores. The scoreboard advances by two points as the team heads down the court high-fiving each other.

Traditional Teams

- Common goals
- Coordinated activities
- Shared incentives

Restaurant employees form a team with common goals and coordinated activities. The front of the house works with the back of the house to create the best customer experience possible. If the patrons have a great meal with great service, they reward the team with tips and a return visit. The restaurant team shares in the rewards of great execution.

At the beginning of the relationship, the salesperson and the customer are not functioning as cooperative teammates. The only thing in common at the beginning of the relationship is that the customer has a problem that requires attention, and the salesperson has a potential solution. This problem-and-solution connection between the two parties is about all the two have in common at this point. A salesperson's incentive is to sell his products at the highest price and with the most favorable terms. The customer is motivated to drive down the price and acquire more for less. Thus, the incentives of the two parties are also not aligned early in the relationship. The activities that the salesperson and the customer use to manage a sale and purchase are also different. The diagram below illustrates the differences that exist at the beginning of the salesperson and customer relationship.

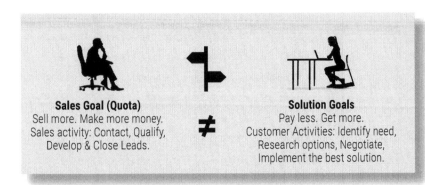

Sales Goal (Quota)
Sell more. Make more money.
Sales activity: Contact, Qualify,
Develop & Close Leads.

≠

Solution Goals
Pay less. Get more.
Customer Activities: Identify need,
Research options, Negotiate,
Implement the best solution.

The Trilogy of Yes calls for cooperation and teamwork to form between the salesperson and the customer. The first step to build a new team with the customer is for the salesperson to welcome the CUSTOMER'S goals as the team's goals. A salesperson can only achieve his goals by addressing his customer's pain points and needs. Cooperating to create winning strategies that achieve the customer's goal is the mission of this newly formed team.

The Trilogy of YES Team
Salesperson & Customer

- Common goals
- Coordinated activities
- Shared incentives

Cooperation and teamwork thrive when both the salesperson and customer march toward a winning solution. Problem-solving is made easy when sellers and buyers work together. Cooperation forms the landscape for a fair exchange of value between both parties. Through cooperation, the salesperson and the customer win together.

Cooperation Is a Part of Us

On my father's 75th birthday, he was diagnosed with a large tumor on his brain, just above the eyes. The tumor may have been 60-plus years old. A few days later my dad had his skull opened and the tumor removed. I have been around a lot of medical procedures and physicians in my life, and I never a saw a more delicate procedure than this one. The precision and teamwork of the surgeon and medical staff was exceptional. My dad, who is an accomplished psychologist, author, and public speaker was shaken by the diagnosis and fearful of the implications of having open-skull surgery, or as I called it, a "skullectomy." Thankfully, the tumor was not cancerous and it was removed without complication.

After his surgery and recovery, my dad took the opportunity to learn more about the human brain. He read books, watched documentaries, and engaged with experts. I shared with him how successful salespeople use cooperation to win, and he said, "Andy, you know our brain is built and organized to leverage the power of cooperation. We are wired as humans to cooperate with one another."

His comment sparked my curiosity. If humans are wired to cooperate, then a salesperson cooperating with a customer is a natural act. I looked for confirmation that cooperation is built into who we are as humans. My research proved my dad right. Neurological studies revealed " . . . one of the most consistent findings has been that cooperative decisions activate brain areas associated with the subjective experience of reward . . . it appears the act of cooperation itself can generate an increase in activation in these areas."[5]

The authors of this study cite three cooperative interactions that elicit brain activation and activity: reward, guilt anticipation, and social ties. In other words, the brain deploys a positive chemical response that motivates us to function cooperatively.

There's more. MRI scanning has shown the brain seeks cooperation. "Mutual cooperation was associated with consistent activation in the brain areas that have been linked with reward processing . . . "[6]

The brain craves cooperation. It's likely that your customer will welcome and be open to your cooperative orientation. Once the customer recognizes that you are motivated by helping her achieve her goals, she will be more likely to cooperate with you.

Marcus Aurelius linked cooperation to human nature when he said:

> We are made for cooperation, like feet, like hands, like eyelids, like
> the rows of the upper and lower teeth. To act against one another,
> then, is contrary to nature . . .[7]

"Co" is together and "operation" is to act. The choice for a salesperson to cooperate is significant. Cooperate and align yourself to the natural wiring of the customer, or work only to achieve your goals and alienate the customer. Blindness to the goals of your customer may engender competition that dampens teamwork. In sales, competition between the salesperson and the customer creates friction, as each party stays focused on defending its turf. We think about competition in black-and-white terms. There must be a winner and a loser, us against them. In this polarized situation, we can't form a team. On the contrary: we don't want to compete against our customer. Rather, we want to strive to form a high-functioning team together.

I believe even Charles Darwin, who preached a philosophy of "survival of the fittest" in nature and capitalism, would recognize the important role of cooperation in sales. If Darwin wrote about great salespeople today, maybe he would say, as I like to phrase it: "The strongest salespeople are those who find ways to cooperate with their customers."

Cooperation with your customer is as important as arriving to the first meeting with him on time. If you are late to the first appointment, you may get the sale, but you begin the engagement at a deficit. Further, the late-arriving salesperson opens the meeting with an apology, "I'm sorry for being late." "Sorry" is not the second word you want to mutter to a prospective customer. Why would you be late? Why would you make the sale more difficult by having to dig out of a hole?

Cooperation works the same way. If you choose to take a different approach with your customer, the deck will be stacked against you. If your competitor is cooperating and you are not, I am putting my money on the competitor to win. Also, be cautious and avoid situations that may appear to be cooperative yet actually undermine teamwork. I have seen good salespeople unknowingly alienate customers by practicing uncooperative sales techniques:

Sales Action	Intent	Result
Good Salesperson, Bad Company Approach.	The salesperson tries to partner with the customer by deflecting bad news on his company. "I would love to do this for you, but corporate won't let me."	The customer observes that the salesperson does not have the authority to make decisions. The customer wonders, "Can I trust someone who is disloyal to his own company?"

continued on page 40

Sales Action	Intent	Result
The Title Jockey Approach (only care about the decision maker at the top).	The salesperson ignores key influencers and stakeholders in the buying process as he only focuses on the person with the most senior title in the organization.	A chorus of negativity comes forward from purchase influencers who complain about the salesperson's tone and approach. The senior leader rebrands the salesperson as an opportunist.

Here's a helpful mantra to use, "Never be late. Always cooperate!"

Compete with the Competitor, Not Your Customer

I am a super competitive person. I hate losing more than I enjoy winning. I love sales, because each selling opportunity is a unique challenge. Having a competitive orientation is a helpful sales strength. However, to me, the challenge isn't about how to maximize my paycheck, it's about navigating a dialogue that ends with both parties saying YES and shaking hands. The competitive aspect of sales occurs when you pivot a difficult customer engagement into a productive partnership. Salespeople compete by turning customer challenges into opportunities. Opportunities transition to successes and result in great commissions and earnings.

Focus your competitive enthusiasm into customer service excellence. "If I do my best work with the customer, the competition will have no chance to take this sale away from me." Top salespeople and sales leaders sell at their best when they face a competitive obstacle such as a rival product. The "win or lose" sense of urgency that takes over pushes these salespeople to become hyper-focused on the needs of their customer. When competitors try to persuade the customer, the salesperson who has built the strongest customer trust and partnership has the advantage. Cooperate with the customer, compete against the threat of losing the sale to the competition. Make your customer's goals yours. Maintain the customer's best interests as you advocate for the benefits of your products.

Let's look at an example that brings together the three skills of The Trilogy of Yes to illustrate how connection, communication, and cooperation work in harmony with one another. As I share this example with you, I'll ask you to consider a moment in your sales career when you formed a team with another person to solve a problem or advance an agenda. Think about how you felt when you established a strong rhythm and problem-solving cadence with your customer. The genesis of these feelings is likely rooted in cooperation. My goal is to create a win-win for you and your customer. Your customer wins through your advocacy and the product solution you provide. Once this occurs, you win the sale, the commission, and the relationship equity that comes from a job well done. By forming a cooperative team with your customer throughout the sales cycle, you increase the likelihood of achieving a winning solution for all parties.

Connecting, Communicating, and Cooperating to Get the Deal Done

Having led multiple sales teams, I had the opportunity to jump into contract negotiations that were heading down the wrong road and help get them back on the right track. An old boss of mine would often say, "When you are the leader, the issues that make it to your desk are the most complex and hairy of all. That's why you've been asked to get involved." He was right. A line I like to deploy when more junior people in the organization push back on the advice of senior sales leaders is: "Those at the top of the sales organization likely got there because they were the best salespeople in the company." It's a thoughtfully worded way to suggest to the regional sales manager that the leader may have insight and perspective that may make a difference.

The big, wonky sales situations are the fun ones. One was a real barn-burner. A large hospital buying group, notorious for very strong and aggressive negotiating, approached me with a new contracting opportunity. I wanted to win with this buying group because of its power to drive high market share to the preferred vendor.

The contract negotiation began with 50 pages of customer terms and conditions. My team, at this point, was totally in the dark as to what the buying group's true needs were. It wasn't clear what the customer wanted to achieve and how our products were perceived by the key stakeholders in the buying group. The good news was that the buying group had historically purchased our products and wanted to do business with us under a more organized and structured contract. It sought to harmonize price, confirm after-sale support agreements, and extract greater savings while committing to purchase more.

The sales leader spearheading the discussions got our legal counsel involved to try and negotiate the terms. Now, as a sales leader, I love working with lawyers. Lawyers have helped me thoughtfully structure contracts that provide favorable terms and conditions for the company. However, getting lawyers involved early in a contract negotiation, before cooperation is established, often opens Pandora's Box. When a customer hears "get legal involved," fears go through the roof. In this negotiation, progress had ground to a halt.

I was asked to jump in and help get the negotiation unstuck. I looked at who the stakeholders were in the discussion. It was interesting. In addition to the buying group, an outside firm was also present. The buying group had begun to outsource its after-sales support to less expensive third parties. It became clear to me that the third party on the phone was a power player in this negotiation. For progress to resume, I needed to drive cooperation and alignment with the third party.

The first negotiation call I joined was with the customer, the third party, my team, and a bunch of lawyers. It was a bloodbath. The lawyers were terse with each other, and our team was defensive. The buying group was quietly fuming before becoming openly frustrated at the lack of progress we were making. There was little cooperation. The only two positives I took away from the call were:

1.   Surprisingly, with the level of acrimony I experienced on the call, most customers would have simply walked away from the

negotiation table. However, the customer continued to engage. This positive buying signal gave me reason to believe a deal was possible.

2. If we established a connection and cooperated with one another, we might generate momentum and sign a winning deal.

At the post-call debrief with my team, I suggested, "Let me take the next action item. I don't want anyone else talking to these folks until we change our tone and approach. We won't make progress with conflict."

I figured out how to create a breakthrough in the negotiation. I had to connect with, and build cooperation with, the third-party customer. If I could get them advocating for this contract, we might get this negotiation moving. I only had the first names of the third-party team members who were on the phone call. I went to the company website and tracked down their contact information. I found senior leaders and started emailing and calling them. Quickly one of the leaders replied and directed me to a new guy at the company who appeared to have a lead role in business development. I phoned this individual and the call went like this:

Andy: "Tony, hi this Andy Olen calling. Our two companies are engaged in a challenging contract negotiation with the hospital buying group. I was hoping we could chat for a few minutes and try to problem-solve. Before we get going, I noticed you went to Marquette University. I grew up in Milwaukee."

Tony: "Milwaukee? I loved living in Milwaukee."

Andy: "Wow! That is awesome. I went to the University of Wisconsin. You guys had our number in basketball last year."

Tony: "It's a great rivalry."

We continued to talk about my hometown and his journey from Milwaukee to his current role. After establishing a rapport and a connection, I pivoted to cooperation and the business at hand.

Andy: "I wanted to reach out to you and see if it would be possible for us to get to know each other a bit and put on the table our shared opportunities and concerns. What can I do for you that would get this negotiation back on track?"

The customer's goals and interests became my priority.

Tony: "That's great. It's actually pretty simple: we need to have access to the after-sale support program in order to be able to fulfill our contractual obligations to the buying group."

Andy: "Okay, I can make that work if you would be willing to help us move the total contract forward. We both have a shared interest in seeing this succeed. The faster we sign, the sooner we enjoy the benefits of this deal."

Together we created the win-win solution.

Tony: "Let's get this program completed soon. We all want this to happen."

The two of us got the ball rolling. We acknowledged the challenging issues on the table, and there were a few items we had to iron out. However, the work was now being done by two guys who both had a connection to Milwaukee and had a fun rivalry to chat about. This connection engendered cooperation and in return accelerated problem-solving. As we solved the support component of the contract, the rest of the negotiation opened up quickly. We pivoted to a more robust negotiation on terms, market share, and pricing. I handed off the rest of the trading to a skilled leader in our organization who cooperated with the customer until the ink was dry on the final contract. We won a multi-year, multi-million-dollar deal that took our pricing up as the customer committed to buy more!

This is an example of what I call Tilting the Sale. Tilting the Sale is the phenomenon of selling more then you planned AND your customer is happy about buying more than planned. The salesperson's ability to Tilt the Sale is the reward for successfully deploying The Trilogy of Yes skills. Progress was made when the customer and I established a connection, communicated openly, and agreed to work cooperatively together to drive the negotiation forward.

Cooperation and Teamwork Accelerate Success

I say to my sales teams, "Strong teams solve big problems." There is no such thing as an "easy" sale. I've never experienced the following:

> *Andy:* "Hello Mr. Customer. It's nice to meet you. Will you buy my product for $5,000?"
>
> *Customer:* "It's nice to meet you too. Yes! Where do I sign? Can I pay you cash right now?"

If it ever gets this "easy," that's the end of the selling profession. Customers face complex problems and have unique challenges. Their needs change fast as their business demands increase. Your ability to put yourself in their shoes and understand their pain points is paramount. When you become an advocate to help them achieve their goals, you become an ally and teammate. Once aligned, you form a team that problem solves and works toward meeting the customer's goal. Your advocacy for the customer pays a healthy dividend. When you combine cooperation together with connection and communication, you move your customer to YES. When the customer gives a confident YES to you, it means she achieved her goals. And when she wins, you win too.

Part 2

APPLYING THE TRILOGY OF YES SKILLS

Connection, communication, and cooperation are the Trilogy's three sales skills that inspire your customer to say YES.

With the bedrock principles of the Trilogy in hand, let's apply these three skills to the sales cycle. A sales cycle is the combination of selling and buying activities executed over time that lead to a potential purchase and possibly a long-term partnership. The Trilogy of Yes sales cycle focuses on building profitable and durable relationships with customers. Relationship building with customers parallels life. With years of experience in living life, your Trilogy of Yes sales training has already begun. There are three phases to the sales cycle.

Phase 1: Dating. In this phase, we begin the customer relationship. We seek to discover similarities and establish a connection. We work to uncover the customer's pain points and needs. In the Dating Phase, we connect and plant the seeds of cooperation. We deploy communication that helps form the early bonds of the new relationship.

Phase 2: Trading. This is the time to negotiate. The key here is to leverage the connection that you built in the Dating Phase and pivot into a cooperative negotiation. We will walk through proven approaches that allow you to always say YES to your customer as long as you ask for value in return.

Phase 3: Partnering. This phase of the sales cycle is designed to transition the relationship with the customer from a single sale to a multi-deal, long-term sales relationship. The relationship that you built in the Dating and Trading phases is leveraged into a partnership. Your connection deepens with existing customers and expands to new stakeholders. A cooperative team works together to address business opportunities while communication helps solidify the solution-focused partnership.

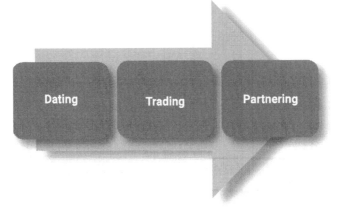

The Trilogy of Yes is not only about getting your customer to say YES to a purchase, it's about creating an environment that inspires the customer to say YES to big deals. By deploying the three sales skills of connection, communication, and cooperation across the three phases of the sales cycle, the salesperson may be able to Tilt the Sale. Tilting the Sale is the explosive upside result that occurs when a salesperson sells more than expected to a customer motivated to buy more.

Chapter 4

Tilting the Sale

"Great things are done by a series of small things brought together."
— *Vincent Van Gogh*

The Trilogy of Yes creates a unique and explosive selling opportunity. I call it Tilting the Sale. Simply stated, Tilting the Sale occurs when the salesperson sells more than she expected as the customer energetically buys more than he had planned.

Here are three types of successful Tilts:

- Add a Zero to the Value of The Sale: A talented saleswoman in Canada working for a major web media company turned a $70,000 product offer into a $700,000 purchase. Adding a zero to the sale is a unique event. Each zero added is a 10 times multiplier to the value of the sale and hopefully to the commissions check as well.

- Adding Years: A salesman negotiated a major contract from an initial offer of $2,000,000 a year for *three* years to a final program worth $3,000,000 a year for *five* years.

- Adding Products: The music store salesperson successfully added an annual three-year tuning contract, 10 lessons, and an upgraded bench to the sale of the baby grand piano.

- Adding Profit: The thoughtfully incented salesperson guided the customer into an upgraded vacation package that delivered improved profit margins for the company.

Tilting the Sale is not a strong-arm pressure play by the salesperson toward the customer to buy more. Rather, the uniqueness of Tilting the Sale is that the customer is willing and wanting to buy more. Strong execution of the three Trilogy of Yes sales skills positively motivates the customer to increase the size of the purchase.

To illustrate a Tilt, let's reverse roles and recall a moment when we as the customer said the following, "Boy, I didn't plan on spending this much." We've all been here. Buying a home often leads to the following statement: "We went over our budget!"

One of two thoughts and corresponding emotions follow the over-budget sentence:

> "We got a great deal and more features than I expected!" Satisfaction, optimism, confidence.
>
> "I'm not happy about this." Anger and frustration.

The difference between the two emotions—excitement about spending more than budgeted, or frustration about overspending the budget—boils down to the effectiveness of the salesperson guiding the customer to the positive feelings. When connection, communication, and cooperation are used in concert with one another, the salesperson has a shot at selling more than her original offer.

Conversely, when a customer believes he is making a bad decision, fear returns. Sometimes customers will still say YES and buy. When this happens, the salesperson may be rewarded with a short-term win, but she will not build a lasting partnership with this customer. The fear of having made a bad decision will push the customer away from the salesperson.

A successful Tilt sounds like this, "Boy, I didn't plan on spending this much, and I'm glad I did. I love my new home!" In fact, there is often a gleefulness about breaking the budget a bit because there is a conviction the best deal was won and the extra dollars spent were well deployed. The confidence and excitement deployed by the salesperson energizes the customer to want

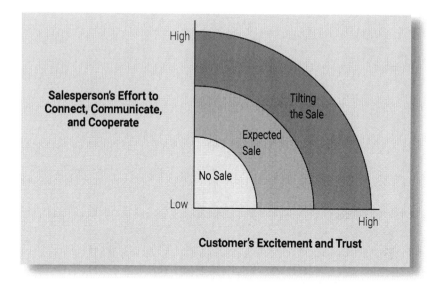

to buy more. A Tilt is a mutually beneficial win-win and is unlocked through the effort and approach of the salesperson.

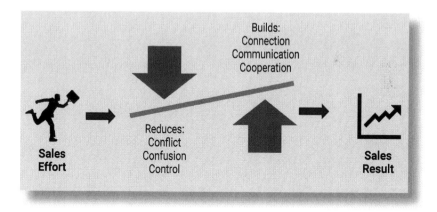

When a Tilt is achieved, it is strong validation that your sales approach resonated with the customer. When the customer energetically adds to the sale, know that the work you put into your sales skills has paid off.

Chapter 5

The Dating Phase

"When you meet someone for the first time, that's not the whole book. That's just the first page." — Brody Dalle

I'm watching my sixth-grade daughter take on the challenge of middle school. Using lockers for the first time, hustling down the hall to get to the next class, earning letter grades, and starting to "date." Well, it's not "dating" in the sense that we know it. Nobody is driving to pick up a date and going to the movies. Dating in sixth grade goes like this: A boy likes a girl, and tries to find her cell phone number. Next the boy texts the girl and asks if they should "date." The girl says yes, and they are an item. It all starts in sixth grade. Buckle up, parents.

The dating dance is the process we use to find the right partner. Some dates go well and others not so well. I had a chance to "date again" in my 30s. I was divorced at 34 and re-entered the dating scene in Toronto, Canada, where I was living at the time. I was curious about meeting new people, and enjoying the restaurant and social scene in a vibrant city. Quickly I saw parallels between the process we go through to meet other people in life and the early encounters we have with new customers. Thus, the first phase of the sales cycle is the Dating Phase. Deploy The Trilogy of Yes skills while "dating" your customer and maximize your chances to earn a second meeting and move the engagement toward a sale.

The Objectives of the Dating Phase

The parallels between real life relationship-building and developing a rapport with a customer are numerous. In real life, after the first date, there is a decision whether or not to proceed to a second date. The second date may consist of dinner and a movie. The getting-to-know-each other progression continues from there. Although there may not be a marriage proposal on the second date, the stakes start to rise. "Will you join my parents and me for brunch this weekend?" "My cousin is getting married, and it would be great if you could meet my friends and family. Will you go?"

The customer Dating Phase likely doesn't include brunch with the parents. It does, however, include significant levels of discovery about one another. The seeds of connection are planted and nurtured during the Dating Phase. The customer will signal his desire to continue to a second meeting. The willingness to accept an offer to buy the product will be made clear as the Dating Phase evolves.

There are three sales objectives to accomplish in the Dating Phase:

1. Build trust with the customer by establishing a connection,
2. Uncover the challenge or pain point the customer is facing that requires a solution, and
3. Ask questions that uncover the customer's goals, and motivations.

By the end of the first meeting, position the customer to say YES to a second meeting or, if the Dating Phase objectives are achieved, to accept the Starting Point Offer. The Starting Point Offer is the first formal purchase request the salesperson makes to the customer.

The Salesperson as Trust Broker

Trust management is a big business. I'm not talking about the kind of financial and fiduciary management that puts assets under the watchful eye of a trustee on behalf of beneficiaries. I'm referring to the big business of helping people manage trust and confidence between two parties. For example, look around at the tremendous infrastructure that has been built to broker trust between buyers and sellers. Institutions have been established to serve as trust intermediaries that facilitate the financial exchange of products for a payment.

For example, eBay rates its sellers to transmit confidence to the buyer that the purchased product is as advertised. The auction website evaluates whether sellers have a strong track record of selling products. The stronger the eBay score, the more we trust buying from this seller. PayPal is a trust broker that moves payments between parties. We trust PayPal to facilitate the transfer of money in return for goods and services sold. Banks sell financial products AND trust solutions. "I will safely hold your money for you, and when you decide to buy something, I will process the funds from your account to the receiving party, who confidently awaits payment."

A salesperson serves as the trust broker between the customer and the business' product. I recently bought a microphone because I wanted to record some guitar riffs. I investigated microphones on the Internet before going to the store. However, my knowledge of brand preference was limited. At the store, I looked at all the microphone options, yet had no way to trust what was good or what wasn't good.

| Customer | Trust | Product |

The store salesperson approached and educated me on the multiple products and options. The salesperson became the trust broker between me and the product I ultimately purchased. His opinions confidently guided me to a product solution.

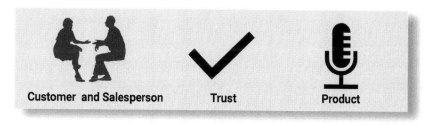

| Customer and Salesperson | Trust | Product |

Salespeople serve as the bridge between the customer and the product. As the customer develops trust in the salesperson, trust in the product increases. A well-known sales truth is "customers don't buy products, they buy the people selling the product." Therefore, salespeople serve as a trust broker, bonding the customer to the product. By connecting and finding a common link, the first helpful "=" equal sign, trust begins to form in the Dating Phase.

Establishing the First Connection Accelerates Trust

I once walked into a hospital operating room department at a well-known U.S. hospital to visit with the program director. I began the meeting by asking the customer introductory questions. I wanted to know who he was, where he was from, and why he chose his line of work. At one point, I shared I was from Milwaukee, Wisconsin. He asked if I was a Green Bay Packer fan, which I am. He pointed to the top of his bookshelf, where a Green Bay Packer helmet was sitting. I grinned as we connected. Not only did we share the same favorite football team, I learned the customer also worked at a Wisconsin hospital I knew well. These connecting moments allowed us to find common ground quickly. As I rotated the conversation to medical products, I watched the customer's body language relax as he opened about his opportunities and challenges in the hospital. Trust began to form within minutes of meeting this customer for the first time.

Another memorable example of establishing a first connection occurred when I toured a military hospital with a Brazilian general in Rio de Janeiro. He was proper and formal. He asked me to salute the nurses and the doctors greeting us. We had never met, and I was concerned it would take some time to win this customer's trust. He continued to be formal and direct until I spotted a guitar in the corner of his office and shared with him that I also played. He picked it up, played, and sang "Imagine" by John Lennon. His formal disposition was replaced with music and an immediate connection formed. His hard exterior softened as stories of music began to dominate the early conversation. To play an instrument and sing in front of another person requires confidence and trust. The general oozed confidence, and our connection over music engendered trust. Suffice it to say, we made great sales progress together.

Make it your goal to quickly find a connection with the customer. Scan the room and look for pictures, books, awards, degrees that reside on the office walls and bookshelves. One of the first things I look for in a customer's office is a personal item. If it's publicly displayed, it's fair game to ask a question.

"Ah, I see you went to UCLA. How was that experience? I bet it was amazing."

"Is that you and your family on vacation? Where did you go?"

Good to Great. I have that book on my shelf as well."

"Wow, did your kids draw these pictures? How old are they?"

Establishing a quick and early connection in the Dating Phase creates trust and a common link that turns a potentially awkward first encounter into a productive and sincere engagement.

Apply the Golden Rule

The Dating Phase accelerates as the salesperson establishes a connection with the customer, and eventually uncovers how his product will address the customer's needs. Like dating in the real world, we likely don't share all our deepest thoughts and "most interesting" insights on the first, second, or even the third date. As trust grows, we open up and share more about ourselves.

In the Dating Phase, practice appropriate connectivity with the customer. Remember, you are in a professional setting. You are seeking to trade a product for a payment with another person. Fears are heightened at the beginning of the Dating Phase because trust has not yet been established. Some customers may be over-revealing early in the discussion to assert authority or manage the trepidation of a first meeting. Regardless of the customer's approach, it's important for you to always recognize that you are operating in a business setting.

Here, appropriate connectivity is measured using the Golden Rule approach. The Golden Rule states: "Treat others in the same way you would like to be treated." Put yourself into the customer's shoes. When I am the customer, how do I want salespeople to approach me? Personally, I want people to respect my time, inquire about my needs, be comfortable in their own skin, and manage a discussion without it being awkward. I don't want someone to "sell me." I want someone to partner with me to find a solution to the challenge I face. Reciprocate these same sentiments back to the customer through your actions. Think about how you want the customer to engage you in a business setting and then act in a similar manner in return.

Communication in the Dating Phase

If we hope to keep dating someone, it's advised that we communicate in a manner that brings the other party closer. How many times have you heard a friend say, "I went out on a date and the person talked the whole time about himself." Does your customer want to hear only about you during the first meeting? Likely not. The difference in The Trilogy of Yes process versus real-life dating is that the goal is to have the customer talk and share the entire time. To positively activate the customer, we must choose encouraging words, present welcoming body language, and ask questions. It's critical to exit the Dating Phase with as complete a picture as possible of what motivates the customer AND why he is seeking a new solution. Once a connection is made and trust begins to form, understanding his motivation for buying a product is critical to insure that our initial offer lands favorably. If we miss the mark here, then we will struggle to articulate a helpful solution. Specific communication techniques help us achieve our Dating Phase objectives.

"You," the Dating Phase Pronoun

Use the pronoun "you" in combination with open-ended questions or requests as much as possible in the Dating Phase. Remember, now in the sales cycle, it's all about the customer opening and sharing:

> "Tell me about YOU."
> "Where did YOU grow up? Tell me about your hometown."
> "YOU mentioned in your email that your budgeting period ends at the end of the calendar year. Can YOU tell me more about that?"
> "Thank YOU!"

Open-ended "you" questions ease the customer into the flow of the conversation. "You" questions also help uncover the first of many shared connections. Open-ended questions lead to multi-word or multi-sentence answers versus close-ended questions that yield one-word answers. The more the customer reveals, the more likely multiple connections will be made. You may discover a friend you have in common, a shared favorite musical genre, a favorite sports team, a similar ancestry, or that you both share the guilty pleasure of keeping up with the highs and lows of *The Bachelorette*. Use "you" to engage the customer early in the Dating Phase.

Words and Sentences that Build Trust and Maintain Momentum

In addition to the power pronoun "you," there are a series of words that work well in the Dating Phase. Words express emotion. For example, the following statement conveys an implied feeling: "Thank you for meeting with me today. I know your time is valuable, and I appreciate that you are spending this time with me." Acknowledging the customer's time signals respect and care for a limited resource. The table below provides a list of words and phrases to use during the Dating Phase along with the desired emotion and feeling we seek to transfer to the customer.

Dating Phase Words	Express
"You have many options, and I appreciate that you are considering my product." "It is a pleasure to meet you."	Gratitude
"I've been looking forward to this meeting." "I'm optimistic I can provide a solution for you."	Optimism
"I'm interested to hear more about what you do in your role." "If you don't mind, talk to me about the key initiatives you are working on." "If you would share with me your knowledge and impressions of my product, that would be helpful."	Interest

continued on page 60

Dating Phase Words	Express
"You do amazing work here." "I get energized about meeting with folks like you and trying to help solve a problem."	Passion

Proceed by Asking Discovery Questions

After asking strong introductory questions that get the customer talking, ask discovery questions. The answers to these questions will help shape the Starting Point Offer. Discovery questions help the salesperson better understand the needs and pain points the customer is facing. In addition, discovery questions provide insight into the customer's motivation/incentive to find a winning solution. The customer may have been asked to buy a product that helps improve the company's profit. If the acquired product delivers on this goal, the customer receives a larger bonus. As the salesperson, understanding these important cause-and-effect relationships will help you position your product offering in relation to the customer's goals and incentives. Examples of helpful discovery questions are:

Discovery Questions	Targeted Insight
"Can you share with me what motivated you to learn more about my product?" "Can you explain how my product may help you?"	Understand the customer's challenge.
"What benefits and improvements are you seeking from the product?" "Share with me, if you would, how you will evaluate success once you move forward with a solution?"	Understand how the customer benefits from a solution.
"In the past, how have you and your department been recognized for achievement?"	Understand how the customer personally benefits from a solution.

Open-ended discovery questions work in both a business-to-business and a business-to-consumer sales environment. When selling to consumers, replace the goals and incentives of the business with the goals and incentives of the consumer. For example, young parents purchasing a car may be motivated by the safety performance of the automobile. The incentive for these parents is to keep their children safe and secure. This discovery helps the salesperson position the car's safety benefits first.

Body Language in the Dating Phase

It's important that the salesperson's body language match the words shared with the customer. We've all been in a meeting when someone says the right words, yet we see this person is clearly checked out and uninterested in the conversation. We hear words; we see body language. Therefore, when we see and hear the same positive messages delivered together—it connects. Body language is important in the Dating Phase of the sales cycle because we want to make a strong first impression. The customer will watch and observe our body language. We want the entire picture presented to be positive and enduring. Below are body language best practices that have proven to be effective in the Dating Phase of the customer engagement.

Maintain steady eye contact. You are watching your customer to learn more about him. He is watching back, and will interpret your eye contact as interest and engagement.

Your posture matters. Here are two different postures that send two different messages to the customer:

1. A salesperson leaning forward toward the customer, nodding in agreement as the customer speaks. Shoulders are broad and raised, and the elbows are on the table.
2. A salesperson with arms folded, sitting back in the chair, and eyes wandering as the customer speaks.

The first example illustrates an engaged and interested posture. The second posture shows disinterest and an aloofness that won't connect. Your body language must remain consistent with your words. Let your posture showcase strong engagement.

Become the learner. Imagine yourself as a student in college. Do you remember the kid who always sat in the front row of the lecture hall? He took a lot of notes and asked a lot of questions. Although it may have been a tad annoying to those of us sitting in the back of the room, it's a recommended approach to use with your customer. In your Dating Phase customer meetings, play the role of student in the front of the class as you engage your customer early in the new relationship. Be vulnerable in front of him and welcome new insights and ideas.

Capture and retain your customer's ideas and opinions throughout the meeting. Take notes with pen and paper. No matter my sales title, I always pull out a pen and notebook to gather notes and impressions. Note-taking sends a signal to the customer that you care about what he says. These notes will also be used during the creation of the Starting Point Offer as you look to tie the customer's needs and incentives to the benefits of your product offering.

Avoid Communication Shortcuts

We live in a world that has grown to accept the use of shortcuts. We type instead of write a thank-you note. We drive through Starbucks rather than walk inside to pick up our coffee. FYI: we have np w/ abbrv. words rather than spelling them out. (Translation: For your information, we have no problem with abbreviating words.) Instead of calling someone to say we're excited to go to dinner, we reply with a thumb's up emoji in a text message.

In sales, and arguably in life, shortcuts should never become substitutes for the impactful and important role interpersonal skills play in building a customer relationship. Voice the customer's name throughout the meeting. Don't use obscure company or product jargon or acronyms unfamiliar to the customer. Confirm with him that your response answered the important question asked. Write a handwritten thank-you note whenever possible. Doing it the "old fashioned" way matters. Our goal throughout the sales cycle is to maximize the power of connection, communication, and cooperation. Don't take shortcuts when the extra interpersonal effort pays a healthier dividend. Our language, both words and body, is the strongest sales tool we have. No product brochure will ever connect more than we will through the words we choose and how we amplify these words with our body language.

Cooperation Engages the Customer

Forming a cooperative team with the customer helps both parties address and solve challenges. Teamwork doesn't magically develop when two people meet for the first time. To begin the process of forming a team with the customer, the salesperson must deliberately engage in team-building activities. I'm not suggesting that you take your customer to a ropes-and-ladders course and do trust-falls. Rather, use both communication and cooperation best practices to build teamwork with the customer. Interestingly, improvisational comedians offer helpful insights on how to form powerful teams.

The interplay of the comedic actors with one another on stage is how they make the audience laugh. Although the comedians are unaware of the skit's subject matter, they are guided by comedic strategies that help transform any topic, no matter how bland it is, into comedic theater.

Let's first look at how an improvisational skit is born. As I mentioned, the comedians do not know what the topic of the skit will be until they are standing together in front of the audience. For example, the master of ceremonies (M.C.) informs the crowd that the new game, or skit, is called "mash-up." She asks the crowd to "Suggest a fun form of entertainment." The crowd yells back ideas:

Audience: "Going to the movies." "Sporting events." "Concerts."

The M.C. chooses a "concert" and continues:

M.C: "Who is performing at this concert?"
Audience: "Red Hot Chili Peppers" "Lady Gaga." "Barney the Dinosaur."
M.C: "All right, it looks like Barney the Dinosaur will open for Lady Gaga."

She asks her final question, "What venue is the concert going to be performed in?"

The crowd, now getting giddier, knowing that something fun will happen, yells:

Audience: "Red Rocks!" "Central Park!" "White House State Dinner!"

The M.C has all she needs at this point and sets the scene for the comedic team, "Comedians, Barney the Dinosaur is opening for Lady Gaga at the White House State Dinner honoring the German Chancellor. Steve, you are the red-carpet reporter interviewing the guests walking into the White House who can't wait to see tonight's unique concert. And . . . Scene!"

Off we go as the skit begins. The inputs create a canvas, and the improvisational comedians shape the story. The actors work together as a team to bring the scene to life. The more they cooperate, the bigger the laughs.

How do they work together so effectively? How can they think of funny things to say or do when they just learned about the content of the skit for the first time? Although the content is new, the comedians are ready to perform because a common framework binds them together. These comedians practice teamwork skills with each other before performing in front of a crowd. They are trained in the following techniques:

- Serve the other.
- Got your back.
- Don't steal the scene!
- "Yes, and"

In the Dating Phase, the salesperson doesn't have the luxury of a trained customer reciprocating helpful team-building skills. However, the salesperson who develops effective team-building skills, similar to these improvisational comedians, will be able to effectively use and enjoy the benefits of creating a cooperative environment with the customer. Using these approaches, the salesperson elevates the customer's goals, motivations, and incentives to the forefront of the discussion. Let's take a deeper look at the comedic team-building skills and apply them to the Dating Phase.

Serve the other: When both comedians are in service to the other, they do everything possible to set their teammates up to succeed. They know that teamwork yields a better performance than the work of the solo artist. By serving the other performer and having that service reciprocated, the actors shine in front of the crowd.

Sales Application: The salesperson is in the service of the customer (customer service). Make the goals and incentives of your customer your priority. Take a "I'm here to serve you" mindset into your early interactions with the customer.

Got your back: In improvisational comedy, you support your teammate. You pull your teammates up when they fall and encourage them to keep moving forward. Just as strong buildings are supported by reinforced steel beams, an effective improvisational team is cast with comedians who defend and encourage their teammates.

Sales Application: Always insure that the customer feels supported. No question the customer asks is naïve or silly, and if you sense he is uncomfortable at any time, it's your job to help navigate the discussion back to his comfort zone.

Don't steal the scene: Improvisational comedy is a team event, and there is no lead player. I call it "peacocking" when someone steals the limelight in front of teammates. This person gets up in front of the room and fans out his feathers for everyone to admire. Peacocking won't get you too far in team comedy.

Sales Application: Listen intently and don't talk over your customer. I know we get excited to talk about our products and our solutions. However, the Dating Phase is all about listening to the customer. You may have the most interesting array of products to sell, and have been trained to do it well. However, avoid "bag diving" and overwhelming the customer with product detail. The time will come when you will have a chance to offer deeper insights and opinions. Don't let your first or second impression with the customer be suffocating. Avoid becoming the peacock.

"Yes, and" is an effective storytelling approach. "Yes, and" mandates that the comedians take all new ideas and build on them with a supportive response

and additive comments. *"Yes,* of course Elvis is still alive, *and* I heard he is Barney's special guest tonight!" "Yes, and" responses build momentum. "Yes, and" is the opposite of "Yeah, but." While "Yeah, but" erodes a cooperative discussion, "Yes, and" builds a productive engagement.

Sales Application: Use "Yes, and" with your customers to keep them engaged and sharing. "Yes, and tell me more about your recent promotion. What did you accomplish to earn this new role?"

In the Dating Phase, apply the tactics and methods of comedic cooperation to build teamwork with your customer. Try "got your back" or "Yes, and" approaches. They're positive in nature, proven effective, and motivate the customer to create a team with you.

The Game Plan for Your First "Date"

When you are prepared, it is easier to relax and connect. When you are unprepared, you play from behind, and burn calories just to keep pace with the customer. A lack of preparation can turn into defensiveness when you are challenged. Customers may interpret defensiveness as a protective shield guarding something within. The likelihood of forming a connection and a cooperative team decreases as your shield goes up. Therefore, good preparation gives you more confidence and the ability to be quietly confident in front of the customer.

I'll share a preparation approach I used with physician customers. I'm not a doctor and will never treat a patient. I didn't go to school for 15 years to practice medicine. I appreciate selling to doctors because I must be well prepared to sell a product I couldn't use on a patient myself. Physician customers, like all customers, deserve our preparation. Whether you meet with a doctor or a business executive, or take a customer appointment at a neighborhood business, a few simple activities will help you prepare for the engagement:

Step 1: Gather research on the customer in advance of the meeting through the web, including LinkedIn, Instagram, Facebook, and Twitter. I also enlist the help of, and perspectives of, others who already know the customer I am to meet with. My goal, prior to the first meeting, is to establish a composite of my customer that helps me prepare my introductory questions.

Step 2: Prepare your questions. In addition to preparing the discovery questions, I prepare questions and conversation starters to better appreciate what it's like to walk in my customer's shoes. For a physician, how does it feel to treat patients? What emotion and positive outcome is felt when a doctor saves a patient's life? I find most people are natural teachers and like to talk about both what they do, and the joy they discover through their work. Guiding the customer into a teaching style, with you as the attentive student, will help you better position your products and offer.

Step 3: Next, ask the customer to illustrate what a good and bad day at work looks like. Doctors gave me insight into the pain points, thrills, and spills of work in a hospital setting. Be prepared to hear about the customer's day in detail. Often you will walk away from this portion of the conversation learning something that can be applied in the negotiation or later as you meet a broader group of customer stakeholders that influence decision making.

Step 4: Seek to uncover the customer's hobbies and passions. I want to learn about my customers as parents, travelers, teachers, readers, pilots, and Ironmen triathletes. These insights create reconnecting moments to use the next time you see your customer. "It's great to see you again. Tell me how your Ironman Triathlon went."

Step 5: Prepare to gather the customer's insights on products and technology. With doctors, I want to know why they chose certain products for certain cases. By this time, you have gathered all the demographic and connecting information needed to establish the early relationship. The product and technology discussion is an important moment to collate the customer's opinions about the pros and cons of both your product and the competitors'.

Step 6: Edit, or be aware of, your social media content knowing that customers will also be researching you. Customers can cancel a meeting with you at a moment's notice without any reason if they learn something about you that leaves them uncomfortable. Ask yourself the question: "Would you be comfortable having your grandmother or young child consume your social media?" If you answered "no," then you might want to make some changes. Don't let social media push your customer away. As you seek to cooperate and effectively communicate, keep your 2010 spring break photos offline. Don't lose a sale with divisive social or political posts on Internet media. Don't push away your customer due to your late-night escapades showcased on Twitter. Be thoughtful about what you share. Your bonus may depend on it.

Having a plan in place before the meeting will help you relax and be more yourself during these critical first moments. There will be no awkward pauses as the relationship accelerates off the launch pad.

Achieving the Dating Phase Objectives

In the Dating Phase, we set out to:

1. Build trust with the customer by establishing a connection,
2. Uncover the challenge or pain point the customer is facing that requires a solution, and
3. Ask questions and uncover the customer's goals, and motivations.

Deploying the skills and actions of The Trilogy of Yes throughout the Dating Phase helps accomplish these three objectives. The salesperson serves as the broker to create trust between the customer and the product. The salesperson seeks to connect early with the customer and generate a spark of trust. Thoughtful communication is used to ease the customer, get her talking, and collect information and insights that motivate action. With cooperation, you form a team that elevates the customer's goals and incentives to the center of the engagement.

The Dating Phase ends when you have gathered enough information to prepare your Starting Point Offer. Continue the Dating Phase if you do not have enough data to build your first offer, or if you sense that your customer is not ready to move onto the Trading Phase. It's important that both of you are ready to move forward together. Be patient: the bigger the opportunity in front of you, the longer the Dating Phase may last. Also, sales cycles will be different across industries and markets. Some cycles are short while others are long and require that multiple relationships be formed prior to the first sale made. I've "dated" a customer for two years before we began negotiating. Once both parties are comfortable and ready to move forward, the Trading Phase begins.

In life, we date in search of building a lasting relationship. We exercise many of the same patterns and approaches with customers. Deploy the skills of The Trilogy of Yes in the new relationship with your customer, and you will be well prepared to formally offer your products with assurance that your Starting Point Offer will hit the mark.

Chapter 6

The Starting Point Offer

"When you're prepared, you're more confident. When you have a strategy, you're more comfortable." — *Fred Couples*

All great beginnings have a starting moment. The eventual gold medalist in the 100-meter sprint readies on the starting line. A great movie has a powerful and captivating start to the story. A boundless life adventure starts at birth. All great sales negotiations kick off with a Starting Point Offer. The Starting Point Offer acts as the transition point from the Dating to the Trading Phase. This offer represents the salesperson's formal request of the customer to purchase a product. Once presented, the negotiation follows.

One of my former colleagues from Quebec, Canada, would say, "We must fingerprint the offer and negotiation." In other words, an effective sales activity is to gain insight into, and an understanding of, the customer's needs prior to presenting him with the first offer. The activities you executed in the Dating Phase gave you these needed inputs. Thus, a proposal is fingerprinted when the Starting Point Offer addresses nearly all the customer's needs. Let's look at two examples of Starting Point Offers. The first illustrates the consequences of being caught surprised and unprepared; the second showcases the benefits of being well-prepared with the first offer.

Never Be Caught by Surprise

A salesperson had a $1,500,000, three-year deal arise with a major customer, who sought to upgrade from desktop computers to portable tablets. Unfortunately, the salesperson had not maintained a close relationship to this large account. He was caught by surprise when a customer in the account he hadn't met indicated he was soon to buy. The customer called the salesperson and asked for a quotation, indicating that she had multiple vendors under consideration. The salesperson did not have the time to run a proper Dating Phase. He was forced to issue a Starting Point Offer without insightful preparation.

A week after mailing an offer, the salesperson was called in to meet with the customer and review the program. The meeting did not go well for the salesperson. Without connection, communication, and cooperation established, the entire conversation turned to price. The Starting Point Offer was out of phase with the customer's expectations and the competitive bids. The customer quickly turned the salesperson into the "price pawn"—that is, the customer sought to lower the price with the pawn and use the lower price as negotiation leverage with the stronger competitors. Ultimately the salesperson lost the deal before it started. Two important items were missed:

1. The salesperson was not connected to this customer—the two clearly never "Dated," and
2. The Starting Point Offer missed the mark completely.

Without proper inputs and preparation, the Starting Point Offer was dead on arrival. Worse, the salesperson ended up playing the role of "price pawn" and wasted time in a losing negotiation.

A Fingerprinted Offer Creates More Value

A salesperson spent two years working with, and building, a close relationship with a customer in a large company. The salesperson was aware of a long-term, multi-million-dollar opportunity working its way forward. The salesperson ran a successful long-term Dating Phase operation. Dating Phase activities included the leadership team of the company meeting with the customer and providing new educational opportunities for his staff. When it came time for the multi-year contract to be bid out, the salesperson was in an excellent position to fingerprint the Starting Point Offer.

The salesperson did a great job addressing the needs of the customer in the Starting Point Offer. Encouragingly, the customer came back with an interesting first negotiation question. He asked, "Can you raise the price? I will work it out that everyone will bid higher so more value can be exchanged on the front end." The customer wanted to pay MORE to get a broader program done. The salesperson won the business at higher prices and increased volume. This is an example of how a strong Starting Point Offer, coupled with a well run Dating Phase, can lead to Tilting the Sale.

The moral of both stories is: the closer you are to your customer, the stronger the Starting Point will be, and the negotiation will begin with you in position to score a win.

Preparation and the Starting Point Offer

Perfect preparation makes for a perfect start to a negotiation. By the end of the Dating Phase, you should have all the raw material you need to create a strong Starting Point Offer. It's time to process the raw material and prepare the bid.

I recommend preparing the Starting Point Offer using the following eight-step approach:

Step 1. Put the data and inputs on the table—literally! Find a quiet location and bring together all of your customer notes, price lists, product brochures, and a few blank sheets of paper. Spread all of the information out on the table. Give yourself 30 uninterrupted minutes to organize your inputs.

Step 2. Answer the following question: What pain points and needs are encouraging my customer to act? Take a blank piece of paper and write down your customer's needs. Scribe a list of words and ideas the customer shared. Pain points and needs may be big or small. A CEO of a Fortune 100 company may be under pressure to improve the brand image of the multibillion-dollar firm. Or, the entrepreneurial graphic designer may need a vibrant local advertising campaign to start to spread the word on her young business. Following is an example of a salesperson listing her customer's goals. The customer is responsible for improving the company's inventory management approach and the timely shipping of products to end users.

Customer's Pain Points & Needs

- Inventory management is broken and costs are increasing
- Too many backorders
- Customer care receiving many angry customer calls

Step 3. Answer the following question: What are my customer's goals? On a blank piece of paper, write down your customer's goals.

Customer's Goals

- Build a just-in-time manufacturing process
- Reduce inventory costs
- Increase the fill-rate on orders that will improve customer satisfaction

Step 4. Marry the inputs from Step 2 and Step 3 to create a customer mosaic. Match the customer's pain points to the goals, and draw lines across the page when certain problem/solution themes come together. On a new page, create the customer mosaic. The template for the mosaic is:

Customer Mosaic Template

My customer is _____.
                    <List Pain Points & Needs>

Her goals are _____.
                    <List Goals>

Once the goals are achieved, _____.
                    <List incentives and rewards>

The completed mosaic for the inventory management customer provides a brief and concise description of her pain points, goals, and incentives:

> **Customer Mosaic**
>
> My customer is having problems controlling inventory costs, has too many backorders and as a result has unhappy end users. Her goals are to improve customer satisfaction and reduce costs by building a new manufacturing process. As the goals are achieved, my customer and her team will be rewarded with a large end-of-year-bonus.

Step 5. Take your brochures, products, prices, and programs and identify the product solution you intend to offer. The product selections you make ideally will create a solution that aligns to the customer mosaic.

Step 6. Write down your Starting Point Offer outline on a fresh sheet of paper. Challenge yourself to create two or three different packages or programs for the customer. Once written, validate that your offer aligns to the themes in the customer mosaic.

> **Starting Point Offer Outline**
>
> Just-In-Time Manufacturing Solution
> - Benefits
> - Pricing
> - Terms
>
> Inventory Management Solution
> - Benefits
> - Pricing
> - Terms

Step 7. Prepare Your Starting Point Offer. Use the outline as a guide to fill in the detail of the offer. The Starting Point Offer may take the form of a product quotation, a formal answer to a Request for Proposal, or simply a verbal explanation of the proposal.

Step 8. Engage a thought partner and ask him to review the offer with you. A thought partner is a trusted confidant to share ideas with and receive feedback from. A good thought partner will provide new ideas and challenge your thinking to make it stronger. "Yes, I love this, and I think you could add that." A thought partner may be a sales manager, a colleague, a spouse/partner, a friend, or a family member. Personally, I like engaging thought partners who have experience in the same market I do. Their informed feedback adds depth to the Starting Point Offer.

Presenting the Starting Point Offer to the customer depends on the format that has been requested. If the customer has indicated that an in-person presentation is required, then the Starting Point Offer may evolve into a slideshow accompanied by a written summary. Sometimes a customer will simply ask for the detail by email. In this situation, approach the customer and make a request for an in-person meeting to review the offer. The power of being face-to-face with the customer dwarfs the impact of an emailed proposal. If the customer will only accept email, write a clear and concise email hitting the main points of your bid and make a request for a live meeting to answer the customer's questions.

Make the presentation of the offer your own. We have been focused on creating an authentic connection with the customer throughout the sales cycle. When preparing the Starting Point Offer, it's important for you to use words and language true to your personality. Let your best be on display by presenting a thoughtful and clear Starting Point Offer. When effectively executed, a strong Starting Point Offer kicks off a cooperative negotiation.

Chapter 7

The Trading Phase

"The wise man puts himself last and finds himself first." — Lao Tsu

It's time to negotiate! In the Trading Phase, the salesperson and the customer jockey back and forth seeking the best conditions for buying and selling a product. The salesperson attempts to sell the product for terms favorable to her while the customer seeks to buy the product for terms favorable to him. The Trading Phase is a rich and animated exchange. Requests are made and emotions may run high. The Trilogy of Yes approach calls for further deploying connection, communication, and cooperation to successfully create a mutually beneficial outcome.

The relationship with the customer transitions from Dating activities to Trading activities. Personal relationships also evolve from a Dating Phase to a Trading Phase. The discussion of the personal relationship moves from getting to know one another to planning a life together. The relationship negotiation begins.

"I would like kids. What are your thoughts on having children?"
"If we spend Thanksgiving with your family, can we spend Christmas with my family?"
"I love cats. Let's talk about your idea to adopt a dog."

These relationship discussions are important. Couples who can maintain a close connection, communicate, and cooperate come together to make life-shaping decisions. When trust is high, good decisions are made, and both people in the conversation exit optimistically and more committed to one another.

Obviously the relationship with our life partners is different than the relationships we have with customers. Instead of discussing which pet to raise together, the discussion with the customer focuses on buying and selling:

"The competitor's price is lower than yours. Can you do better?"

"Can I get a rebate if I add volume to this order?"

"Are you open to accepting our terms and conditions?"

Navigating the Trading Phase with our customers is hard work. When done well, the results can be tremendous.

The Objectives of the Trading Phase

There are two objectives in the Trading Phase:

1. Create a cooperative negotiation that leads to a sale, and
2. Seek to Tilt the Sale.

The Trading Phase is the opportunity to create a win-win for both parties. Tilting the Sale occurs during the Trading Phase. The salesperson's ability to transition a conflict-based negotiation into a fair and cooperative discussion gives her momentum. Tilting begins with this subtle momentum shift. Momentum delicately moves to the salesperson without the customer feeling like he is "losing" ground in the negotiation. In fact, the customer grows more excited because he believes the product offer improves as the negotiation moves along. A Tilting of the Sale results in a happy customer saying YES to buying more. As we discussed earlier, a Tilt benefits the customer and returns a HUGE win for the salesperson.

Cooperation in Action throughout the Negotiation

I have been asked numerous times by friends and family to help them negotiate a new car purchase. I ask why they need help. The response is the same: "Oh, I just don't like negotiating. I feel like I am going to get pushed around.

It's too much conflict." Behind these reasons there is a simpler explanation. The reason people don't like negotiating is that we fear saying and hearing "no." "No" is uncooperative, it runs counter to our DNA, and it does not engender teamwork. "No" activates emotions such as disappointment and frustration. "No" signals rejection and failure. Negotiations have the potential to become challenging moments filled with wide-ranging emotions. Maintaining cooperation is not easy as tensions increase. The following are a few examples of the negative consequences that arise out of a negotiation that is moving sideways.

Negative Negotiation Moments	The Threat to Cooperation
Customer vents frustration about the cost of the product.	Salesperson becomes defensive and antagonizes the customer.
Customer won't decide.	Salesperson becomes impatient and pushes the customer to act.
Customer threatens to buy a competitive product.	Salesperson criticizes the customer's reasoning.
Customer pushes the purchase to a later time.	Salesperson fears quota may be missed.

I understand why people seek to avoid negotiations. The fear of conflict and rejection is a powerful force. The good news is that we can overcome these roadblocks and anxieties. A negotiation can be successfully managed without conflict and rejection. By establishing a cooperative foundation with the customer in the Dating Phase, and continuing to cooperate in the Trading Phase, we curb conflict and promote teamwork. Cooperation is conflict's antidote.

Moments arise in the negotiation where conflict, frustration, and an unwelcome request may push the negotiation off the tracks. In these moments, try to re-anchor the discussion in cooperation. Pushing back with a negative response or a conflict-creating position accelerates the breakdown of cooperation. The negative cycle of negotiation conflict looks like this:

The salesperson has the power to break the cycle of negotiation conflict. She must identify the conflict and appropriately respond to keep cooperation intact. This sales skill requires nimbleness and agility. Here's a conflict to cooperation cycle that helps keep the negotiation moving forward.

Tips and Tricks to Maintain Cooperation through the Negotiation. If the negotiation turns toward conflict, or you sense it is moving in a negative direction, there are a few easy adjustments that will re-orient the discussion back to its foundation of teamwork. Here's how to keep cooperation in play throughout the negotiation.

Tip 1: Listen and Observe. Active listening and observation underpins a
    cooperative negotiation. Customers give us signs all the time. Listen
    to their tone, inflection, and words for early clues if a tense moment is
    coming. Body language changes indicate a challenging moment may be
    approaching.

    Here's a tip: if there are two customers in the room, watch both
    closely. I was in a negotiation once and the primary customer was
    pushing hard on a few points. However, his colleague sitting next
    to him was giving me all the answers I needed as I observed his
    body language. I asked, "Are we competitively priced?" The primary
    customer said, "No!" Thankfully, his colleague was nodding "Yes," and
    that was the answer I needed. Most people aren't gifted poker players.
    Watch their body language for clues.

Tip 2: Think Cooperation. Always Be Cooperating. Here's a new ABC
    acronym to add to the sales dictionary along with Always Be Closing.
    When the going gets tough in the negotiation, ask yourself, "How
    do I respond with cooperation?" Before responding to a tough
    question, take a moment to think it through. It's best to pause and
    think about a cooperative response rather than to blurt back conflict.
    Always attempt to take the high road. Your customer teammate has
    a challenge. How can you help him solve it? Think first and speak
    second.

Tip 3: Ask a Question. Respond to your customer by acknowledging
    his concerns and asking a question. This helpful approach gets the
    customer talking and saying more. Often the customer will voice his
    preferred solution while responding to your question.

Tip 4: Problem-Solve. Invite the customer to problem-solve with you. Seek a joint solution: "How should *we* tackle this problem?" Or try "What would a good solution look like to you?" Rather than abruptly blocking the customer's challenging request, capture the momentum of his energy and pivot the discussion by acknowledging the challenge and replying with a problem-solving question or statement. In a tough negotiation, turn the negative energy of conflict into positive problem-solving.

Communication Facilitates a Cooperative Negotiation

Remember our Power Sentence? Here it is again:

"YES I CAN IF TOGETHER WE WIN."

The Trading Phase features the first four words "YES I CAN IF."

Continue to Say YES

In the Trading Phase, the customer will make multiple requests. He may ask for a price discount, free shipping, and extended payment terms. You can say YES to every one of these requests "if" you ask for something of value to you in return. Continue to role model the words you want to hear from a customer by using YES in response to each of the customer's requests. However, in the Trading Phase, YES must be accompanied by a few more Power Words in order to maintain equity and fairness in the negotiation.

Introduce the Pronoun "I"

We used the pronoun "you" in the Dating Phase. In the Trading Phase, rotate to, and use, the pronoun "I."

"I appreciate your willingness to buy this product."

"I wanted to review the offer in person with you."

"I understand the key items you are interested in. Let me call those out for you in the proposal."

It is appropriate to detail and defend your Starting Point Offer. "I" helps frame the offer and clarify your key positions in the negotiation. This is your offer, and you can stand confidently behind it with the use of "I" statements.

"Can" Moves the Negotiation Forward

"Can" is a verb that denotes action. "I can" informs the customer that you are ready to move. As trading requests are made by the customer, the ability to reply to each request with "I can" creates progress. The opposite of "I can" is the uncooperative "I can't" which will grind the negotiation to a halt. Use "I will," a more declarative version of "I can," when there is no question that you can deliver on the commitment.

"If": A Little Big Word

"If" may be the most important word in the Trading Phase. "If" allows the salesperson to answer "Yes, I can" to the customer's request and then ask for value in return. "If," when joined with "Yes" and "I can," works like this:

"Yes, I can provide free shipping IF you deliver the purchase order today." "Absolutely. I am able to provide a discount IF you purchase two units." "I am happy to look at an early payment discount IF the total purchases exceed $10,000."

"If" gives the salesperson the ability to say YES to every request as long as the customer agrees to trade value in return. Voicing "Yes, I can" continues the cooperative exchange; "if" maintains equity and fairness between the salesperson and the customer. "Yes, I can if . . ." responses should be used frequently. "Yes, I can if . . ." is not just a great negotiating tactic, it's a great sentence to use in trading situations, big and small, in real life.

Use Customer-centric Financial Terms

I've been in many negotiations where the salesperson uses the wrong financial terms with the customer. The salesperson shows a slide that is titled "Revenue Over the Last 12 Months." Revenue? Revenue is what the seller's company recognizes, not the customer. The customer designates the purchase of a product as an expense. Don't speak of a customer's purchase as "revenue," use the word "investment." Investments are made and investments return value. It's beneficial to use financial terms as long as they are oriented to the customer's perspective.

Connecting Words to Positive Outcomes

There are four positive outcomes we want to create during the negotiation, and we unlock these results through the words we choose. Next are examples of sentences and phrases to use with the customer, and the positive outcomes they create.

Trading Phase Sentences	Positive Outcomes
"I appreciate you taking the time to study the proposal. I know this is a large investment for your company. Do you have any questions I can answer?" "I understand your request. I think we can work toward a solution." "I know you have budgetary constraints. I created a few scenarios in the offer to address your concerns."	Acknowledgment: Validate the customer's request and concerns.
"I am confident we can work this out together." "If I can move on price, are you able to get the needed sign-offs completed this week?" "I will go to bat for you in this deal if you are willing to go to bat for me as well."	Cooperation and fairness.
"I'm pleased we are making progress." "I like negotiating with you because you are clear about your needs." "I believe we have made tremendous strides. Are you comfortable with where we stand today?"	Momentum toward completion.
"I have a few small points left to ask about." "I think we are all done. Is there any open issue or topic you want to visit or re-visit?" "We have worked everything out. I think we have a deal."	Completion: Seek an end to the negotiation.

Body Language through the Negotiation

Body language in the Trading Phase mirrors that of the Dating Phase. Continue with professional and engaged body language throughout the negotiation. Avoid body language and facial expressions that signal frustration and impatience. As discussed earlier, negotiations have the power to easily open divides between the salesperson and the customer. Avoid these trap doors by maintaining neutral body language.

This is a struggle for many, especially for me, because I am very expressive. My face shows excitement and frustration. People who know me well recognize when I am energized because they see it in my expressions. Because I have become frustrated in negotiations in the past, I work hard to maintain a neutral bias in these moments. I relax my face and try to listen as intently as possible to the customer. Shifting my energy toward listening has helped me maintain a calm face.

If you sense frustration levels rising for your customer, it's okay to address it head on by saying, "I sense you are getting frustrated. If so, is there something I can do to help?" Break the ice, ask about the concern, and provide solutions to work through the tough moment. As the customer replaces frustration with engagement, there likely will be a solution found to the problem. Monitoring your body language and keenly observing your customer's helps move the negotiation forward.

Maintain Your Customer's Respect

The connection developed with the customer in the Dating Phase creates the bond and rapport needed to effectively navigate a cooperative negotiation. However, don't fall into the false assumption that your pathway to winning a sale is simply based on the customer "liking" you.

Likeability is important throughout the entire sales cycle. However, during the Trading Phase, it is important that likeability does not block sensibility. I have witnessed many good salespeople give away too much value because they wanted to only please the customer. A former colleague and I would ask, "What's more important? A happy customer or a happy company?" The answer must always be both.

That said, salespeople sometimes struggle asking for value from the customer. Some believe the easy thing to do is to say YES to everything the customer wants without asking for anything in return. These salespeople will do anything to avoid the dreaded customer "no." They are afraid of damaging the "relationship" if they push back. "I don't want to hurt our relationship." The problem with this approach is that savvy customers take advantage of salespeople who are pleasers. Customers extract price concessions by playing on the salesperson's inability to ask for and hold value in the negotiation.

The urge to always be liked must be replaced with the goal to be respected. The successful effort you put forward in building a connection and a cooperative team gives you the ability to say YES to the customer without being taken advantage of. Using "Yes, I can if . . ." language allows you to remain cooperative through a challenging negotiation. Remain cooperative and likeable by saying YES. More importantly, preserve respect and equity in the negotiation by using "if" as a condition to accept a customer's request.

When It's Okay to Say "No"

There may be a moment in the negotiation where you need to say "no." Although "no" appears to run counter to cooperating with the customer, it is a parachute you may need to deploy under certain circumstances. For example, if you are asked to do something illegal or unethical, respond with "no." Also, it is okay to deploy a "no" or "maybe now isn't the time to negotiate" if the customer's requests become obtuse. If a customer asks, "I would like the product for free, no questions asked," it is okay to say, "You know I can't do that."

You are at the negotiating table for one of three reasons:

1. The customer intends to buy your product,
2. You and a competitor are the finalists for the sale, or
3. The customer does not intend to buy your product and is using you as a negotiating pawn to drive down the price of your competitor's offer.

If you discover you are the pawn, walk away from the negotiating table and let your competitor take the business at the highest possible price. You don't want to pawn your way into a lower price market by negotiating your competition down and getting nothing for it.

If the customer is set on a basement-bottom price and refuses to trade value, it's okay to end the negotiation. "I would love to make this work for you. However, I am unable to match the economics in your budget. Had I known this was the total you were able to spend, I would not have submitted a quote or bid that wouldn't hit the mark."

As you gracefully exit the discussion, the customer will either accept the end of the negotiation or balk and say, "Wait, wait, there may be a way for us to make this happen." Shrewd customers and buyers will push you all the way to the edge. It's possible that only voicing a "I-can't-continue"-type line will you get to the truth. If the customer is trying to negotiate with you far below your Starting Point, bowing out gracefully maintains fairness in the relationship and likely preserves access for re-engagement at a later time.

Tilting the Sale as the Negotiation Closes

A Tilt begins to show itself as the investment of connection, communication, and cooperation begin to pay off. The customer's initial fears are replaced with optimism. The salesperson's communication style in the Dating and the Trading Phases has connected, and the customer has opened up. Trust deepens toward the end of a mutually beneficial negotiation. The salesperson's consistency and predictability is paying dividends. It is at this moment when a Tilting opportunity arises.

As The Trilogy of Yes actions take root in the Trading Phase, the salesperson may sense she has negotiation momentum. If momentum is present, it's time to ask a Tilting Question. A Tilting Question is a test question for the customer. It's a verbal trial balloon that is meant to gauge his interest in purchasing more. The customer's answer to the Tilting Question informs the salesperson if selling more remains a possibility. Here are a few examples of Tilting Questions:

"We are nearing the end of the negotiation. The program we put together is strong. I know that you are looking to buy more units over time. Would you consider buying one of those extra units now under the terms we just negotiated?"

"You are really close to a purchase amount that gives me the opportunity to kick in some value-added items. Do you want to explore how to get there?"

"Now, I know we are negotiating a one-year deal. I have flexibility on rebates if you are open to a multi-year program. Is that something we can discuss today?"

I have four tips to help the salesperson effectively deploy the Tilting Question:

Tip 1: The Tilting Question is asked when the salesperson is confident that the customer is positively energized. If the customer is unhappy with the negotiation, asking him to potentially buy more would be a mistake.

Tip 2: The Tilting Question in no way can submarine the deal on the table. I can hear one of my sales mentors tell me, "When you get the sale, say thank you and get out!" The Tilting Question should be deployed just before a final YES is given by the customer. Do not deploy the Tilting Question after you have negotiated the final particulars of the deal.

Tip 3: In advance of the negotiation, prepare a few purchase scenarios to share along with the Tilting Question. The Tilting Question and the introduction of new buying opportunities is a planned and purposeful action. If the customer is receptive to your Tilting Question, be ready to offer incremental solutions. Don't bumble your way through an important moment by being unprepared.

Tip 4: Insure you can deliver on the Titling scenario if the customer says YES. Have the incremental offer preapproved by your manager. It would be a cataclysmic outcome to Tilt the Sale and see the final details of the deal rejected at the home office.

The customer answer we want to the Tilting Question is "Yes, tell me more about this," or, "I might be able to do something, and I'll need your help to make it happen." When a customer warmly responds to the Tilting

Question, the salesperson should reveal one of the prepared incremental scenarios. A savvy customer who trusts the salesperson and believes he negotiated a great program may want to add more to the purchase order. He is thinking, "I'm getting a good deal. This wasn't a bad process. I feel good about the purchase. Maybe I should take advantage of the good work I've done and buy more now." In the moment, uncertainty about the future also works to the advantage of the salesperson. The customer is weighing whether to make additive purchases now versus later when the terms may change. He ponders:

"The terms negotiated may change."

"The price might go up."

"I may not get a service discount later."

When the customer agrees to do more, the sale is Tilted. The salesperson has moved the customer to an almost certain YES on the initial sale. More powerfully, the salesperson lifts the value of the deal above and beyond original expectations using the Tilting Question and incremental scenarios.

We hear about athletes and artists who were "in the zone" when they executed a series of great plays or created an artistic masterpiece. Tilting the Sale feels the same. Sales professionals who execute The Trilogy of Yes and negotiate incremental value versus the Starting Point Offer are "in the sales zone." They transform the great work they did in creating a trusting connection, positively communicating, and cooperating through the negotiation into an explosive sales result. The customer and salesperson both score a big win as the sale is Tilted.

Achieving the Trading Phase Objectives

Our two Trading Phase objectives were:

1. Create a cooperative negotiation that leads to a sale, and
2. Seek to Tilt the Sale.

Deploying the actions of The Trilogy of Yes in the Trading Phase helps the salesperson and customer navigate the negotiation phase of the sales cycle.

The customer's receipt of the Starting Point Offer marks the start of the Trading Phase. Deploying cooperative tactics and effective communication throughout the negotiation maintains teamwork as the back-and-forth of a tough negotiation unfolds. Say YES to every one of your customer's requests, yet maintain fairness by using "If" to ask for value returned. A Tilting question is asked toward the end of a successful negotiation, and if the customer responds positively, you orient the discussion to incremental selling opportunities. When all parties feel confident that a fair and strong deal was reached, handshakes are exchanged, the customer says "YES," and a purchase order is cut. The Dating Phase is now complete, and the salesperson prepares to move to the Partnering Phase.

Chapter 8

The Partnering Phase

"If we are together nothing is impossible. If we are divided all will fail."
— *Winston Churchill*

In the Trading Phase, you closed the deal, and possibly Tilted the Sale. Now, in the Partnering Phase, it's time to turn the first sale into the second, the tenth, and the hundredth. Though each sale has its own unique challenges, selling to an established customer is easier than winning a sale from a new customer. Building a portfolio of repeat customers creates an annuity of predictable sales. With a strong pipeline of sales from loyal customers, the salesperson has time to prospect and start the Dating Phase with new customers. The Partnering Phase is focused on transitioning your customer relationships into profitable partnerships.

The Objectives of the Partnering Phase

The Partnering Phase has both short- and long-term objectives. The short-term objectives of the Partnering Phase are to:

1. Build a protective fence around the customer or account, and
2. Engage your primary customer in "art of the possible" opportunities.

Ideally the Partnering Phase will continue on for an extended period of time as the salesperson and customer work together. The long-term objective of the Partnering Phase is to deepen and extend your relationships, creating loyal customers and engaging the key influencers and stakeholders who surround them.

A while back, I worked in a business where the sales activity was focused on volume quoting. In other words, the team would try to place as many chips as possible on the roulette table, hoping that the ball would drop on one of the bets. The belief was that if the team quoted three times the sales goal, eventually enough sales would be generated to achieve the quota. The average salesperson had quotes out to 20-plus accounts of varying purchase histories. Some customers never bought from us, while others had purchased only once in the past three years. As the market crowded with competition, repeat customers started moving away from the team. It became clear that this approach was inefficient and generated only transactional customer relationships, not durable partnerships.

Good salespeople efficiently manage their time. They prioritize opportunities that help them achieve their quota. Why seek out a new, small account when a large loyal customer has the potential to add new products? To boost overall territory performance, loyal customers saying YES to repeat purchases is a great way to underpin overall territory growth.

Here is a striking set of sales numbers that illustrate how powerful a small set of loyal customer partners can be if you Tilt the Sale with them through the Partnering Phase. Assuming one loyal customer represents 10 percent of a salesperson's total annual sales, it only takes *two* loyal customers growing 25 percent in a year to raise the TOTAL GROWTH of the full territory by 5 percent.

Loyal Customer Annual Growth %				
# of Loyal Customers	10%	15%	20%	25%
1				
2				***
3			***	***
4		***	***	***
5	***	***	***	***

*** Stay in the shaded area and grow your sales by 5 percent or more each year.

The ability to continue to Tilt the Sale with loyal customers in the Partnering Phase is the most efficient way to grow the size of your total territory. Over time, as you build Trilogy of Yes Partnerships with more and more customers, you will enjoy more predictable sales growth from your territory. Explosive performance will be realized by adding new customers each year to your fleet of loyal buyers.

Your Win Is Somebody's Loss

Throughout my professional career, the counter-punch from a downed competitor has always come 90 days after my team's big wins started rolling. After I helped launch a new product in the U.S. medical field in 2008 that won market leadership in 90 days, the competitors kicked back with new products and highly aggressive offers on price. Their market positions were quickly eroded by our early success, and they devised new strategies to push back on our progress. We were caught flat-footed because we were high-fiving one another in celebration rather than realizing that the competition was drawing up a counterattack strategy.

Monopolist companies, or those who have no competitor, must also fight the pitfalls of relaxing after a big win. "Ah, I just won there. I can move on. I'll go after the next target and check on these guys later." "Lazy monopolist syndrome" is as dangerous as a strong competitor seeking to make a comeback. Either way, attention to, and activation of, the Partnering Phase is critical for defending your gains and pushing new sales forward.

As in the Dating and Trading Phases, there are best practices to use while continuing to connect, to communicate, and to build cooperative teams during the Partnering Phase. However, in this phase, our focus expands and covers two sets of customers:

The primary customer: this is the customer, or sometimes the group of customers, you executed the original sale with. You have Dated and Traded with this customer, and now are building a Partnership.

Stakeholder and influencer customers: these are the people who surround the primary customer and help the salesperson expand her position or defend it from competitive attack. By cultivating a relationship with this group, the salesperson benefits by having a broader team and support network in the account.

Activities to Execute through the Partnering Phase

By this point, you have established a relationship with the primary customer that helped get the first deal done. In the Partnering Phase, expand your relationship with the primary customer, and connect to and build relationships with key stakeholders and influencers that surround this customer.

If you sell to a business, build a defensive shield around the account with the help of key stakeholders and influencers. If you sell to individuals, engage and win over the influencers in their ecosystem. Karen, a general contractor, engaged her client's children to better understand what was important to them in the home remodeling project. Although the customers were the parents, the general contractor was aware that the kids' voices were important as well. A mortgage broker, Jeff, not only worked on securing a good loan for his primary customer, he helped the customer's entire family solve complex financial issues and gave free advice to the customer's friends. Whether you sell to consumers or to businesses, the Partnering Phase of The Trilogy of Yes is the time to insure that the customer who is using the product continues to enjoy the benefits of doing so.

There are four sales actions to take in the Partnering Phase:

1. Follow up quickly with your primary customer after the initial sale.
2. Plant a sales seed for future expansion with the primary customer.
3. Identify the stakeholder and influencer customers.
4. Engage the stakeholder and influencer customers.

Fast Follow-Up with the Primary Customer

We've all taken a victory lap the moment a big sale is won. It's appropriate to celebrate after the successful close of a sale because it feels good and a lot of hard work was put into winning the opportunity. However, as the excitement of the win fades, it's important to re-engage and follow up with the primary customer who is now using the product.

Fast follow-up is a cooperative action. By checking in soon after the sale, you bridge the Trading Phase and the Partnering Phase with your presence and attention. Fast follow-up enables the salesperson to tackle initial problems or address new concerns that may have been raised. You are creating a rapid response mechanism to quickly address challenges and opportunities. Products sometimes don't work as advertised, recalls happen, doubts are put into motion by the competition, a part mis-ships, or the product doesn't turn on.

If you are not present with your customer at these moments because you have shifted your attention to a new account, your customer will become frustrated. The cooperative teaming that had developed previously is in jeopardy. By the time, you re-engage, the customer may be looking for a new solution. Get ahead of problems by being present with the primary customer after the product is purchased.

Plant a Sales Seed with the Primary Customer

A mentor of mine coined the term "the art of the possible." It goes like this: "Let's get creative. Let's push it. Exercise the art of the possible." It was a simple line that usually activated the team to set big goals. I've modified the phrase and ask, "Close your eyes and tell me what winning looks like." The first time you successfully navigate the Trading Phase, a deal has been won. A Tilting of the Sale is an "art of the possible" experience. Now, in the Partnering Phase, the trick is to think about and evaluate even bigger "art of the possible" deals.

To set in motion an "art of the possible" scenario, it's important to first plant a seed with your primary customer that encourages him to envision and begin to justify future investments. The seed is an idea that the salesperson prepares and delivers to the customer. Planting the seed early in the Partnering Phase empowers the salesperson to set new goals and milestones with the customer that will trigger future sales. Like all aspects of The Trilogy of Yes, planting the seed takes a little preparation.

Prior to meeting with your primary customer, prepare purchase scenarios, or seeds to plant, that may be applicable to the situation. Brainstorm and create ideas without limitations. Refer to the notes taken during the initial Dating and Trading Phase meetings for ideas. There often are plenty of insights into additional opportunities that you uncovered throughout the sales cycle. While developing the sales seeds, always keep the customer's goals and best interests front and center. Stay true to the cooperative imperative that the customer's goals remain your goals. Once you have honed in on a few seeds, deploy them with the primary customer using effective conversation starters. Here are a few helpful ways to communicate and plant a sales seed:

Compare your new customer to the company's largest customer. If the largest customer has 10 products in use, politely share this with the new customer who just bought her first product. Illustrate how the largest customer's business has become more successful as more products were purchased.

Create a "when-then" seed. If your product's positive impacts are measurable, prepare a scenario for the customer that asks her to consider buying more as the first product meets or exceeds the measure. "As we discussed, the product will likely improve your productivity by 5 percent. Once we hit the first goal, then we should shoot for a 10 percent productivity gain. How does that sound?" The "when-then" scenario puts in motion a future sale by leveraging the anticipated success of the first product purchase. Early Partnering Phase conversations with your customer open the door to establishing reviewable benchmarks that assist future sales.

Create an "if-will" seed. The "if-will" seed is a cause and effect scenario. "If new funds open up this year, will you consider the following investment?"

Suggest a "let's grow together" seed. This seed tethers your products to your customer's business or personal growth. The seed introduces the idea for the customer that by partnering with you, the business will grow and expand faster. "Your business will grow over the next few years. You invested in your first product to help accelerate growth. Many companies with the same profile as you own five units. I'm excited to help you grow and expand."

A seed is planted early in the Partnering Phase and is watered by the salesperson through reminders and updates. Ideally this seed will eventually transform from an idea into a sale. In the movie *Inception*, the team led by Leonardo DiCaprio's character enters a subject's dream and dives into the subconscious memory, planting an idea that will influence the subject's actions once awakened. Although you don't jump into your customer's dreams, planting the sales seed creates an idea that over time may become a selling opportunity.

Identify New Stakeholder and Influencer Customers

Throughout the Dating and Trading Phases of the sales cycle, you may have identified, met, and worked with a broader set of stakeholders and key influencers who were directly or indirectly involved in the sale. Inventory these people's names, their titles, and their relationships with the primary customer. Ask your primary customer for help and her approval to meet with the stakeholders. Gaining your customer's approval is an important action that maintains transparency and helps navigate personality and political landmines. Build a small action plan for each of these key players in advance of meeting with them.

The action plan for the stakeholder and influencer customers is similar to the work you did in the Dating Phase. In your plan, outline the desired flow of the meeting and the objectives you wish to achieve with the stakeholders. It will be important to gain their feedback on the purchased products, understand their pain points, and evaluate their goals. Stakeholders and influencers may measure success differently than the primary customer. Discovering these insights will help you form a solution-oriented relationship with this important group of customers.

Engage Stakeholder and Influencer Customers

With your plan in hand, schedule time and go meet with the broader customer group. Deploy the Dating Phase tactics used earlier in the sales cycle. The goal with the broader customer group is simple: help them to feel confident about their investment in you and in your products.

Over time, we want to enable a broader group of customers to act as the early warning system when the competition comes calling. This group may also provide a clean transition to a new primary customer if the original is promoted, moves on, or leaves the post. The positive words and actions of these new customers over time helps drive future Tilting opportunities. Their collective voices, in alignment with your primary customer, are more powerful in a chorus together.

An effective tactic to use when expanding the customer base within an account is to pull senior leaders from your company into the Partnering Phase effort. New and powerful connections are made when you offer stakeholders and influencers the following opportunity: "My president wants to thank you for your commitment to our company and our products. Would it be possible for me to bring her here to meet with you?"

In the Partnering Phase, cooperation continues with the primary customer and expands to a broader set of key players. The larger group of customers creates momentum for new purchases. When this group advocates, it creates support for the salesperson and his products. It becomes more difficult for the competition to move in and snatch the business away.

Communication Solidifies the Relationship

The Trilogy of Yes communication approach evolves as we move into the long-term phase of the customer relationship. The key word and concept is "together." It's the teamwork word in the sentence "YES I CAN IF TOGETHER WE WIN."

A product has been exchanged for a payment. The customer is motivated to see the purchase return a dividend. The salesperson seeks to build long-term loyalty and success with the new customer. Everyone is working and winning together. The salesperson's language in the Partnering Phase seeks to create the positive outcome of togetherness with the customer.

Tilting the Sale requires the salesperson to be viewed as a partner and solution provider. "Transactional selling" works in markets where price and volume are the only negotiated terms. On the other hand, "partnership selling" creates dynamic and big wins over the long run. Conditioning the customer by using the word and generating the positive outcome of "togetherness" rotates the salesperson's standing from outsider to insider. It's here where effective salespeople are seen by the customer as part of the team. They create a union and rise together.

Together Phrases	Positive Outcomes
"I'm glad we're together again."	Connected
"My experience tells me we can do more together."	Aligned
"We've come a long way together."	Invested
"I want to see you succeed."	
"We can do this."	
"How can we solve this challenge together?"	

"We," the Pronoun of the Partnering Phase

The Partnering Phase uses the pronoun "we." With cooperation and trust established, it's appropriate to deploy the pronoun "we" with frequency. "We" is plural, teaming, and conveys a union of individuals. Deploy "we" in a positive manner with your customers in the Partnering Phase.

"WE can."

"WE will."

"WE are TOGETHER."

Words and Phrases for the Partnering Phase

"Together" and "we" ought to be deployed frequently with all active customers in the Partnering Phase. To achieve the objectives of the Partnering Phase, voice words that create united and positive outcomes.

Partnering Phrases	Positive Outcomes
"I'm hearing the product has been performing well and the team is happy."	Customer confidence
"I have seen the new products that we are developing, and I'm confident you will be excited about what we are building."	

continued on page 100

Partnering Phrases	Positive Outcomes
"It's great we can sit across the table from each other as partners rather than as salesman and customer." "I want to help you build a solution."	Belief that the salesperson is a solution provider
"Based on what we have accomplished thus far, I see us continuing to have a great experience together." "I know this is a tough challenge we are solving. We'll get through it."	Optimism
"Boy, I'm excited about what we are working on together." "Your company is making great progress. The future looks strong."	Passion
"I hope the experience you had with our company is as strong as the one I've had with yours." "I'm happy to see the product doing well for you. You made a good decision."	Validation

As always, it's important to continue to deploy professional language with the customer. The relationship has developed with the primary customer, and there may be a high level of comfort evolving between the two of you. Convey passion, energy, and optimism while choosing words that are appropriate in a professional setting. Even if the customer uses language with you that is more casual, always keep in mind the professional ecosystem you operate within.

Body Language in the Partnering Phase
I'm a hugger, I'll admit it. When I'm excited to see a customer with whom I have developed a long-term partnership, I express it with a smile and a hug. The Trilogy of Yes works best when you make it your own and incorporate these concepts and suggestions into your personal style and approach. Hug your customer in the Partnering Phase if you are comfortable doing so, and if your customer is comfortable receiving a hug from you.

Body language should be deployed based on the history and connectivity you have with the customer. Align your body language with the primary customer to show a more connected status. Follow the body language tactics you learned in the Dating Phase for stakeholder and influencer customers. Below are additional tips how to effectively use body language in the Partnering Phase:

Engagement: High-engagement body language works well with the primary customer in the Partnering Phase. Leaning forward into the conversation shows interest. Having the pen and notepad out ready to write down a new insight continues to demonstrate care.

Openness: Open your body language to your customer. For example, if you are sitting at a conference table and the customer sits at the head of the table, sit with the chair turned to point toward him rather than toward the table. After saying hello, roll up your sleeves. Speak and listen with your arms open, not crossed.

Touch: Touch can make a difference, and it has to be used thoughtfully. A simple and appropriate touch can go a long way. Chemicals are released in our body when someone shakes our hand or gives us a hug. A simple pat on the back releases oxytocin, a human peptide hormone, that creates a chemical reaction within us that invites trust, warmth, and connectedness.

I've met two U.S. presidents, and at each encounter, I received both a handshake and a pat on the upper arm or shoulder. I vividly remember these encounters and feelings. It's natural for me to shake someone's hand and simultaneously pat the person on the upper arm. Deploy touch if you are comfortable doing so and if the relationship you have with your customer has advanced far enough along for it to be appropriate. When you do this thoughtfully, you may ignite a positive chemical reaction that positively builds the relationship.

Social media: As your relationship advances with your customer, you may be tempted to reach out on LinkedIn, Instagram, Facebook, or Twitter. My advice is to not initiate this level of engagement with a customer. Requesting access to a customer's private or professional digital environment may create anxiety if he is not comfortable extending this space to you. Further, you may put the customer into the awkward position of rejecting your request. Don't initiate the online connection with a customer. It's like playing with a match that may start an unintended fire. If the customer initiates a connection with you, accept it if you are confident that your digital footprint is appropriate to share.

Connecting Continues Deep into the Partnering Phase

You've been appropriately authentic all the way through The Trilogy of Yes sales cycle. Connection and authenticity in the Partnering Phase is simple: continue to be yourself. Trust has been established with your primary customer.

Remaining Consistent and Predictable over the Long Term

Over the long term of the Partnering Phase, a history of trust will form. Try to maintain your cadence of consistency and predictability. Deviating from your established rhythm could turn into a liability. For example, let's assume you are always highly energetic with a customer. The one day you are down may leave the customer wondering "What's wrong with Andy?"

The reality is that there will be times when you are off your game. Great artists all have off days. In these moments, tell your customer it's been a tough day. Be open if you aren't feeling sharp or at your best. The benefit of The Trilogy of Yes approach is that as you build connection and cooperation, you can lean on it when you are in a pinch.

Always Move Forward

In the earlier phases of The Trilogy of Yes sales cycle, connection was deployed in a way that helped facilitate building a trusting and cooperative relationship. As the Partnering Phase begins and endures, it's important to grow and deepen your connection with the customer.

As customers get to know you, it is okay to reveal more about yourself. In this regard, establish a steady pace of connecting with your customers. As they ask for more detail about you and what drives you, they are tacitly expressing their willingness for you to ask similar questions in return. Gauge your customers and when you sense they are ready, ask more detailed connecting questions. Always seek to enrich your connections that build more durable partnerships.

Be Confidently Humble

Arrogance is the killer of the naive salesperson. It sounds like this:

"Don't worry, I've got it."
"My customer loves me!"
"He already said yes, he won't say no."

Bud, a great sales leader, categorizes salespeople and sales leaders as either "great chess players" or "one-move checkers players." The great chess players are always thinking about the move that comes next. If I move my bishop to this position, and my opponent counters by moving the knight to that position, what will I do in response? The one-move checkers player prides himself on the singular move, only to be triple-jumped because he did not anticipate what his customer would do in response. A sales relationship begins with the first sale. The competition is taking note of your success. In the Partnering Phase, continue to anticipate the next move your competitors will make to win back the business. Invest time and energy into planning your customer activities and avoid being put into check by the competition. Become a master chess player, not a one-move checkers player.

The sale was won in the Trading Phase. Your confidence should increase as you have success. Turn confidence into continued engagement. However, maintain the genuine approach that got you to this point. Combine humbleness, or modesty, about your success with a quiet confidence that the approach you are using to connect, communicate, and cooperate is working.

A Partnering Example

Soon after landing a big win with a hospital in Montreal, Canada, my sales team and I took the physician customers to dinner. We started the Partnering

Phase that night. Our goal was to have a discussion with them on how to work together and make this new contract become a great success for all parties. With a new, committed contract and now market share leadership in this account, we had the opportunity to expand our sales by engaging at a deeper level with the broader customer group.

The dinner began by me starting the Partnering Phase discussion:

Thank you for the opportunity to be your partner for the next few years. Your trust in our team and our technology is a responsibility we take seriously. We want this to be a great experience for you. Now that we are partners, how can we dazzle you with this program?

Our objective at the dinner was to gain a deeper understanding of how we could rally the broader physician group to the contract. After opening with gratitude, we sought to gain insight into the passions and desires of our customers. They had grown to trust my team. They knew that we consistently delivered against our commitments. The foundation of trust and genuineness gave confidence to one physician to make a very personal request. This doctor's family roots connected him to South America. He was conversational in multiple languages including Portuguese and wanted to spread his wings of medical influence outside of North America. Moreover, he wanted to speak on behalf of the technology in his family's native language. Although his Portuguese was good, speaking in front of esteemed colleagues in South America was a challenging task.

It so happened, I managed the Latin American business as well as Canadian, so I was able to facilitate a large speaking role for this doctor at a South American conference. He delivered a great speech. His openness and trust in my sales team helped him achieve a personal and professional goal. Suffice it to say, our success in his hospital continued to grow as he and others championed our cause for many years. We Tilted the Sale time and time again throughout the Partnering Phase.

Consistency, predictability, openness, and trust create an environment for people to grow together. Building deeper connections and a cooperative team throughout the Partnering Phase serves as the glue that bond salespeople and customers together as partners.

Achieving the Partnering Phase Objectives

Some of the more exciting moments I've had in life have been facilitated by the great partnerships I developed with my customers.

- I co-piloted a plane with a customer whose hobby was flying.
- I drove a Ferrari on a private course in Montreal with my customer who was a racer on the North American Ferrari racing circuit.

We started these relationships by connecting over coffee at Starbucks (or maybe Tim Horton's), effectively communicating, and forming a cooperative team. However, these unique moments all occurred in the Partnering Phase of the sales cycle.

Throughout the Partnering Phase, the relationship with your primary customer will strengthen. Connection and cooperation evolve as communication triggers positive outcomes about the product and the customer's investment. In addition to improving the relationship with the primary customer, you have identified multiple new stakeholder and influencer customers. This new team of customers will help defend your position and generate momentum for new sales. Selling more to existing customers is efficient and rewarding. Building a strong partnership with your customers protects your business and engenders an environment where explosive sales results and repeat Tilting will occur.

Epilogue

The Trilogy of Yes Is Now Yours

"Through discipline comes freedom." — *Aristotle*

Congratulations! You have made it through *The Trilogy of Yes*. Connection, communication, and cooperation are three sales skills that help you build and maximize your customer relationships. Investing in and practicing The Trilogy of Yes approach allows you to transition relationship skills used in day-to-day life into powerful sales actions to use with customers. Ultimately a great customer relationship must produce sales. The Trilogy of Yes skills and sales cycle are built to create explosive sales results. Tilting the Sale occurs when the benefits of connection, communication, and cooperation resonate with customers. Building strong customer relationships makes it easier for the salesperson to consistently grow and expand sales results and do it in a focused and time-effective manner.

The Trilogy of Yes doesn't need to be challenging or difficult because it relies on you consistently and predictably being yourself. What's natural to do shouldn't be difficult to do. The challenge the Trilogy presents is not one of execution, rather one of discipline. To use these sales skills successfully requires discipline, practice, and thoughtfulness.

Using effective communication at the right time requires disciplined listening skills. Preparation before every customer engagement requires forming the habit. Expressing appropriate authenticity requires the ability to interpret the situation and respond to the customer with thoughtfulness. Practicing consistency and predictability requires staying true to yourself. Cooperating when the customer is being difficult necessitates patience and quick thinking to pivot the discussion. The discipline to stay close to your customers, even after you win the first deal, helps defend your position and grow sales among loyal customers. I know you can do it.

The call to action now is to identify one new customer and start the Dating Phase with him or her. Say "Yes, I can if . . ." to a customer in the Trading Phase and ask for value in return. And kick off the Partnering Phase with a customer who recently bought from you for the first time.

I wish you tremendous success with your customers. Use the Trilogy of Yes sales skills—connection, communication, and cooperation—to inspire your customers to say YES, and don't just win the sale, Tilt the Sale your way.

Endnotes

1. J. Holt-Lunstad, T. B. Smith, and J. B. Layton. "Social Relationships and Mortality Risk: A Meta-analytic Review." *PLoS Med* 7, no. 7 (2010): e1000316. doi:10.1371/journal.pmed.1000316.

2. S. Pressman, S. Cohen, G. E. Miller, A. Barkin, B. S. Rabin, and J. J. Treanor. "Loneliness, Social Network Size, and Immune Response to Influenza Vaccination in College Freshmen." *Health Psychology*, 24, (2005): 297-306.

3. Ethan Kross, Marc G. German, Walter Mischel, Edward E. Smith, and Tor D. Wager. "Social Rejection Shares Somatosensory Representations with Physical Pain." *PNAS*, 108, no. 15 (2011): 6270-6275.

4. Miller McPherson, Lynn Smith-Lovin, and Matthew E. Brashears. "Social Isolation in America: Changes in Core Discussion Networks over Two Decades." *American Sociological Review*, 71, no. 3 (June 2006): 353-375.

5. Mirre Stallen and Alan G. Sanfey. "Cooperation in the Brain: Neuroscientific Contributions to Theory and Policy," *Current Opinion in Behavioral Sciences*, 3 (June 2015): 117-121.

6. James K. Rilling, David A. Gutman, Thorsten R. Zeh, Giuseppe Pagnoni, Gregory S. Berns, and Clinton D. Kilts. "A Neural Basis for Social Cooperation." *Neuron* 35, 2 (July 18, 2002): 395-405.

7. Marcus Aurelius. *The Meditations of Marcus Aurelius*, trans. George Long. Vol. II, Part 3. *The Harvard Classics*. (New York: P.F. Collier & Son, 1909–14).